Creating
Vintage Cards

TweetyJill
PUBLICATIONS
makes you creative!

A TweetyJill Publication by Jill Haglund

Published and created by TweetyJill Publications • Printed in China ISBN 1-891898-06-X

For information about wholesale, please contact customer service at tweetyjill.com or 1-941-377-7720

CREDITS:

Book Layout: Jill Haglund • Book Design: Laurie Doherty   • Editor-In-Chief: Lisa Codianne Fowler
Phototography: Herb Booth, Booth Studio • Photo Stylists: Jill Haglund, Lindsay Haglund and Marilyn Haglund

THANKS:

I want to give a heartfelt Thank you to Laurie Doherty and Lisa Codianne Fowler
for their unwaivering support throughout this project.

Vintage ... I Love Anything Vintage.

I even like the way the word looks and sounds.

Vintage items are imparted with character and value. They give you a rich, warm and lasting feeling, whether or not you know their origins. Perhaps part of the appeal lies in their mystery. Or maybe it's that they have earned their rite of passage in a bygone era and have withstood the test of time. Whatever the reason, vintage items are treasures to hold dear, especially if they once belonged to a beloved grandmother, great grandmother or other special relative.

In our fast-paced world today, e-mail, voice mail, faxes and cell phones have accelerated our lives to the point that some days are a blur. Vintage items seem to not only stop time, but to reverse it! No wonder they grab our attention these days.

Hopefully, you know the feeling of a one-of-a-kind vintage find. While exploring an antique shop you discover a little pair of worn, soft leather baby shoes begging for a squeeze; you feel a desire to pick up and connect with old photographs or to run your fingers through the big jar of genuine, antique buttons.

Looking through my own cherished vintage items, I'm flooded with happy memories. I just love rubbing my hand across the cover of my mother's favorite fairytale, an original printing of "Alice in Wonderland" that first taught me to appreciate line drawings, and opening one of her treasured collections of worn poetry books that allowed me to value the written word.

Embrace the past... just for a moment... that is exactly how someone will feel when
they receive a vintage card made by you, with your own hands.

We encourage you to copy your favorite photos, combine them with treasures old and new, and explore the possibilities. It's easy to get hooked on sending out these unique, fun and personal gifts.

Touch the past, capture it and give it away. Your cards are sure to warm the hearts of all who receive them.

Jill Haglund
TweetyJill Publications

Mon Ami
ROBEN-MARIE SMITH

[INSTRUCTIONS]

Cut and fold black cardstock to make card. Sponge large tag with Butterscotch and Ginger inks. Stamp "Ferris Wheel," postage, "Paris," "Crackle" and "Eiffel Tower" to tag in Pitch Black and Ginger dye inks; add ribbon to tag. Glue scrapbook paper to card front. Leave edges up at the bottom and use double-sided tape to add the printed ribbon. Fold edges under paper and then glue all down to card. Glue tag to card. Stamp men onto cardstock, sponge with dye inks, cut out and add black photo corners; glue to tag. Adhere buttons with Glue Dots.

[MATERIALS]

Black Cardstock (for card): Local Craft Store

Diamond Patterned Paper: Li'l Davis Designs

Checkerboard Paper: K&Company

Black Photo Corners: Canson

Tag: American Tag

Ginger, Butterscotch and Pitch Black Adirondack Inkpads: Ranger Industries

"Crackle," "Eiffel Tower Collage" and "Paris Postal Cancellation" Rubber Stamps: Stamper's Anonymous;

"Men" Rubber Stamp: Stampington;

"Ferris Wheel" Rubber Stamp: Treasure Cay

Colored Ribbon: Local Craft Store

Printed Ribbon: Stamper's Anonymous

Adhesives: UHU Glue Stick; Glue Dots International; Scotch Double-Sided Tape

Other: Vintage buttons

Lady Artists' Club

ROBEN-MARIE SMITH

[MATERIALS]

Kraft and Brown Cardstock: Local Craft Store

Mushroom and Pitch Black Adirondack Inkpads: Ranger Industries

Olive Green Cat's Eye Pigment Inkpad: ColorBox by Clearsnap
"Morris Dancers" Rubber Stamp: Stampington & Company

"Lady Artists' Club" Rubber Stamp: Postmodern Design

Black Mini Brads: Making Memories

Metal Label Holder: Anima Designs

Adhesives: UHU Glue Stick; Glue Dots International

Other: Wrapping paper, sheet music, bay leaves and buttons

Tools: 1/8" Hole Punch by Fiskars

[INSTRUCTIONS]

Cut and fold cardstock to make card. Stamp "Morris Dancers" with Pitch Black ink to kraft panel, sponge front with Olive ink and sides with Pitch Black. Layer to dark brown panel, wrapping paper and kraft brown panel; glue to front of card. Tear and sponge sheet music with Mushroom ink and glue to side of the card at the fold. Stamp "Lady Artists' Club" with Pitch Black ink onto scrap paper; sponge with Mushroom and Olive inks. Glue to front of card and secure metal label holder over it with black brads. Adhere bay leaves and button with Glue Dots.

"Give me a museum and I'll fill it." ~ Pablo Picasso

Always
Remember Love
PATTI MUMA

Floral Collage Paper: K&Company

Hot Press Watercolor Paper;
140 lb. Stock: Local Craft Store

Tan Cardstock: Local Craft Store

Sepia Archival Inkpad: Ranger Industries

Ochre Inkpad: Marvy Matchables

Walnut Ink Crystals: Postmodern Design

Safety Pins: Li'l Davis Designs

Eyelets: Making Memories

Adhesives: Avery Glue Stick; Foam Mounting Tape, Pioneer Photo Splits

Other: Large and small tags (hand-cut by artist), cotton string rubbed with sepia ink, brown fiber, copy of vintage photo and photo scan of vintage doily, spray bottle

Tools: Personal paper cutter, scissors, sponge for inks, eyelet setting tools, craft knife and deckle scissors

[INSTRUCTIONS]

Using ruler, tear watercolor paper to achieve deckled edge to size of 11 2/8" x 7 5/8". Stain both watercolor paper and tan cardstock by spraying with walnut ink crystals dissolved in water; allow to dry. Fold in half to create card.

Cut collage paper to fit length of card and tear on one side for deckle. Sponge deckle edge with sepia and ochre inks and glue to folded edge of card. Cut photocopy of doily and adhere to card. Flip card over and trim edges.

Using eyelet setting tools, place eyelets into front of card, one at each end. Run inked string through the holes and tie behind the front panel.

Take stained cardstock and load into computer printer. Using the "center" setting on the tool bar, generate text (allow plenty of spacing!). Using a tag template, trace around text and cut out tags. Sponge edges with sepia ink. Place eyelet and fibers on large tag.

Place safety pins into small tags and attach to string. Secure with photo splits on back of tags. Trim photo with deckle scissors and then use sponge to age photo edges with inks. Place on card using photo splits. Attach large tag to card with foam mounting tape.

[MATERIALS]

Black Cardstock:
Local Craft Store

Script Paper: 7gypsies

Pharmacy Labels:
Stamper's Anonymous

**Pitch Black Adirondack
Inkpad:** Ranger Industries

**"Lady Faces" Rubber
Stamp:** Renaissance
Art Stamps

Ribbon: Offray

Black Eyelets: Making
Memories

Typewriter Keys: 7gypsies

Adhesives: UHU Glue
Stick; Glue Dots
International; Judi Kins
Diamond Glaze

Other: Old book paper,
buttons, flinch card, lace,
color image and vintage
photograph

Tools: Eyelet Setter
by American Tag

[INSTRUCTIONS]

Cut and fold black cardstock
to make a card. Collage and
glue scrap papers, script
paper, flinch card and images
to a black card base as
shown. Adhere buttons and
old lace with Glue Dots. Add
typewriter word to metal
frame and fill with Diamond
Glaze. Adhere to card when
dry. Punch two holes into
bottom right of card and add
eyelets. Pull ribbon through
and secure.

me
ROBEN-MARIE SMITH

ROBEN-MARIE SMITH

Laughter

[MATERIALS]

Olive Cardstock: Paper Cuts

Pattern Background Paper:
Creative Imaginations

Colored Ledger Paper: Treasure Cay

Vintage Collage Image:
Paperbag Studios

Sticker Words: Bo-Bunny Press

Gold Photo Turns: 7gypsies

Black Mini Brads: Making Memories

Adhesive: UHU Glue Stick

Other: Old book page and
postage stamp

Tools: 1/8" Hole Punch by Fiskars

[INSTRUCTIONS]

Cut and fold cardstock to make a card.
Glue scrapbook paper, old book page
and ledger paper to card front. Cut out
image of children and glue to card.
Peel and stick on word stickers. Punch
three holes into the top of the card
and adhere gold photo turns with black
mini brads. Adhere butterfly stamp to
card front.

*"It's good to wish for and look
forward to the wondrous
things in life" ~ Mary Stewart*

Live, Laugh & Love

ROBEN-MARIE SMITH

[MATERIALS]

Colored Cardstock : Paper Cuts

Collage Paper: Pebbles, Inc.

Vintage Collage Image: Paperbag Studios

Simply Stated Rub-On Words: Making Memories

White Acrylic Paint: Delta

Mushroom Adirondack Dye Inkpad: Ranger Industries

Leaf Rubber Stamp: Fred Mullet

Silk Leaves: ARTchix Studio

Silk Flower and Ribbon: Local Craft Store

Washer Words, Metal Photo Corners Making Memories

Swirl Heart: 7gypsies

Adhesives: UHU Glue Stick; Glue Dots International

Tools: Small paintbrush and 1" bristle brush

[INSTRUCTIONS]

Cut and fold cardstock to make a card. Tear and glue scrapbook paper to folded card. Glue photograph to card and adhere metal photo corners with Glue Dots. Stamp leaf on card using Mushroom ink. Using a dry brush technique*, add white acrylic paint to card.

Add a little paint to the metal photo corners as well. Wrap ribbon around front of card and tie through metal heart. Secure metal heart to page with a Glue Dot. Tie a Washer Word through the middle of a silk flower with ribbon; adhere flower and silk leaf to card with Glue Dots. Apply rub-on words to card at bottom right corner.

*Dry brush technique: Apply paint sparingly to the surface using a dry brush allowing background color to show through.

LIVE.LAUGH.LOVE.LIVE.LAUGH.LOVE.LIVE.LAUGH.LOVE

"Within your heart keep one still, secret place where dreams may go." ~ Louise Driscoll

[MATERIALS]

Measurement Paper: 7gypsies

Brown Stripes Paper: K&Company

Hot Press Watercolor Paper, 140 lb. Stock: Local Craft Store

Adhesive-Backed Typewriter Letters: Nostalgiques by Rebecca Sower/EK Success

Torn Phrases and Die Cut Alphabet Stickers (heart and clock sticker): Life's Journey by K&Company

Standard-Size Shipping Tag and Small Scalloped Tag: Local Office Supply

Sepia Archival Inkpad: Ranger Industries

Ribbon: 7gypsies

Brad: Local Craft Store

Adhesives: Avery Glue Stick

Other: Tea bags for staining paper, color copy of vintage photo and copy of vintage dictionary pages

Tools: Paper cutter, ruler, scissors and sponge

[INSTRUCTIONS]

Tear watercolor paper to achieve 11" x 7.5" beveled edge; fold to make card. Soak two teabags in hot water; stain both sides of card with water and allow to dry. Using the photocopies of vintage dictionary pages, collage the shipping tag. Add a strip of Measurement paper and clock and heart stickers. Thread ribbon through top of tag.

Sponge edges of vintage photo with sepia ink. Mat onto brown striped paper. Using direct-to-paper technique, age scalloped tag with sepia ink. Computer-generate text and place on scalloped tag along with the #3 sticker. Use brad to attach tag to photo.

Use photo splits to place tag onto card at an angle. Glue photo onto card. Press torn phrase sticker over photo.

3 Dreamers
PATTI MUMA

laugh

[MATERIALS]

Pattern Paper: K&Company

Cream and Tan Cardstock: Paper Cuts

Sticker Word: Pebbles, Inc.

Small Jewelry Tags: Local Office Supply

Jet Black StazOn Solvent Inkpad: Tsukineko

Sandal Sea Shells Inkpad: Ranger Industries

"Laugh" Rubber Stamp: Paperbag Studios

Velvet Leaf: ARTchix Studio

Silk Flower and Lace: Local Craft Store

Black Mini Brad: Making Memories

Adhesives: UHU Glue Stick; Glue Dots International

Other: Silk sponge

[INSTRUCTIONS]

Glue cut pieces of various patterned paper to front of folded card made from tan cardstock. Using black dye ink, stamp "Laugh" onto cream piece of cardstock. Sponge with Sandal dye ink and glue to card front. Add mini brad to silk flower; glue flower, leaf and lace to card. Add sticker word to card. Glue small jewelry tags to card near flower. Write on tags if desired.

PARIS
PATTI MUMA

[MATERIALS]

Script Paper, White Cardstock, Manila Folder, Gold Vellum and Standard Tracing Paper: Local Craft Store

Sepia Archival Inkpad: Ranger Industries

Dark Brown Inkpad: Marvy Matchables

Walnut Ink: Postmodern Design

Eiffel Tower Rubber Stamp: Limited Edition Rubberstamps

Eyelets: Making Memories

Brads: Lost Art Editions

Adhesives: Glue Stick and Scotch Tape

Other: Sponge for inks

Tools: Paper cutter, scissors, eyelet setting tools and awl

[INSTRUCTIONS]

Create a card using white cardstock; sponge front with sepia ink. Stain manila folder with walnut ink; allow to dry. Cut to a slightly smaller size of card front. Wrap a strip of tracing paper around the center of manila piece; secure in the back with tape. Add eyelets to top and bottom of strip and carefully rip away center of tracing paper as shown.

Stamp Eiffel Tower with dark brown ink on script paper; sponge edges with sepia ink. Computer-generate "Paris" and print onto gold vellum. Carefully tear and attach to front of Eiffel Tower with brads using awl. Glue script panel to walnut panel and walnut panel to card front.

Once Upon a Time in Paris
ROBEN-MARIE SMITH

[MATERIALS]

Red Printed Paper: K&Company

Vintage Image of Eiffel Tower: ARTchix Studio

Sticker Numbers: Pebbles, Inc.

Bubble Letters: Li'l Davis Designs

Printed Acetate: K&Company

Printed Twill: 7gypsies

Ribbon: Offray

Black Elastic: 7gypsies

Circle Frames: Li'l Davis Designs

Black Nail Head, Metal Swirl and Steel End: 7gypsies

Black Mini Brad and Black Eyelets: Making Memories

Adhesives: UHU Glue Stick; Glue Dots International

Tools: Eyelet Setter by American Tag and 1/8" Hole Punch by Fiskars

Other: Beads

[INSTRUCTIONS]

Tear and glue red collage paper to card front, then glue collage image of Eiffel Tower to card front. Adhere acetate to page using Glue Dots (position where words and twill will be placed). Adhere Bubble Letters to card front with Glue Dots. Add black nail head to end of printed twill. Add a black mini brad through the hole in the steel end; add the silver metal swirl and beads. Glue to the other end of the twill and attach to card. Peel and stick number stickers to card. Punch two holes in the card, one at the top and one at the bottom. Set eyelets in holes and add black elastic; tie ribbon to elastic.

"Life consists of what a man is thinking all day"
- Ralph Waldo Emmerson

Red Snap Card
AMY WELLENSTEIN

[MATERIALS]
Tan Text Paper: Design Originals
"Mille" Script Paper: 7gypsies
Cream Cardstock: Bazzill
Red Velvet Paper: Local Craft Store
Black Dressmaker Snaps: Dritz
Adhesives: UHU Glue Stick
Other: Color copy of vintage photo

[INSTRUCTIONS]
1. Trim photo into an oval shape.
2. Adhere photo to decorative text paper using glue stick.
3. Layer on decorative script paper and red velvet paper.
4. Secure to cream-colored card using dressmaker snaps.

Green Snap Card
AMY WELLENSTEIN

[MATERIALS]
Green Floral Paper: Design Originals
"Mille" Script Paper: 7gypsies
Brown Textured Cardstock and Cream Cardstock: Bazzill
Black Dressmaker Snaps: Dritz
Adhesive: UHU Glue Stick
Other: Color copy of vintage photo
Tools: Medium Circle Punch by Marvy Uchida

[INSTRUCTIONS]
1. Use medium circle punch to punch out photo.
2. Adhere photo to decorative script paper using glue stick.
3. Layer on brown cardstock and green floral paper.
4. Secure to cream-colored card using dressmaker snaps.

Otto
AMY WELLENSTEIN

[MATERIALS]
Brown Floral Paper and Tan Script Paper: Design Originals
Brown Textured Cardstock: Bazzill
Decorative Snaps (Screw Heads): Making Memories
Adhesives: UHU Glue Stick
Other: Color copy of vintage photo
Tools: Eyelet setter and hammer

[INSTRUCTIONS
1. Use glue stick to adhere color copy of vintage photo to brown floral paper.
2. Layer brown floral paper on decorative script paper, then mount on a brown card.
3. Set decorative snaps on the four corners of the brown floral paper.

Grandpa's Adventure

PATTI MUMA

[MATERIALS]

Map Paper: K&Company

Black (for card) and Olive Cardstock: Local Craft Store

Sepia Archival Dye Inkpad: Ranger Industries

Walnut Ink: Postmodern Design

Watch Face: 7gypsies

Metal Phrase: from Li'l Davis Designs

Metal Snap: Making Memories

Adhesives: Avery Glue Stick; The Ultimate! Glue

Other: Copies of vintage photographs, walnut stained vellum cream cardstock

Tools: Scissors, spray bottle, tag template, eyelet setter and hammer

[INSTRUCTIONS]

1. Create a card from black cardstock. Trim olive paper and map paper; glue both to front of card. Mount vintage photo of man onto walnut stained cream cardstock; trim. Adhere vintage picture of scenery and matted photo of man to card (to "age" photo you can burn the edges very carefully).

2. Spray vellum scrap with walnut ink and allow to dry. Attach to the card.

3. Glue phrase to the vellum and clock face to card using the Ultimate Glue.

4. To make the dated tag, computer-generate the date and print onto stained cream cardstock.

5. Position tag template, trace and cut out tag with date in the center. Set snap in tag and glue it to card.

Boston

KRISTY JEDINAK

[MATERIALS]

Tan Cardstock (for card): Bazzill

Patterned Papers: Rusty Pickle, 7gypies and Design Originals

"Boston" Sticker: K&Company

Twist Tie Words: I Kandee by Pebbles, Inc.

"Destination" Sticker: Real Life by Pebbles, Inc.

Tags: Making Memories

Fiber: St. Louis Trim

Metal Clip: 7gypsies

Eyelet: Making Memories

Adhesives: Hermafix Glue Dots; Making Memories Pop Dots

Tools: Sizzix Machine and Fiskars 12-inch Paper Cutter

[INSTRUCTIONS]

Cut tan cardstock desired size and fold in half to make card. Adhere scraps of patterned papers to cover entire front of card in collage style. Die cut tag shape using Sizzix and cover tag with papers and sticker. Slip clip on side of tag and add round tag with Pop Dot. Add "Boston" sticker and twist-tie words to tag. Secure eyelet in opening of tag and embellish with fiber. Adhere tag to front of card with Pop Dot.

Sew Thankful

KRISTY JEDINAK

[MATERIALS]

Tan Cardstock (for card): Bazzill

Patterned Papers: 7gypies and Rusty Pickle

Sticker Words: K&Company and The Paper Loft

Sewing Machine and Thimble Charms: K&Company

Adhesives: Hermafix Glue Dots

Other: Scrabble game piece

Tools: Fiskars 12-inch Paper Cutter

[INSTRUCTIONS]

Cut tan cardstock to desired size and fold in half to make card. Add a variety of cut patterned papers to front of card to create a collage. Add sewing machine, thimble, game piece and words as shown.

100% Authentic

ROBEN-MARIE SMITH

[MATERIALS]

Script and Word Papers: 7gypsies

Floral Paper: K&Company

Vintage Postcard Collage Image: Paperbag Studios

Adhesive Word Sticker: Pebbles, Inc.

Sticker Tag: Pebbles, Inc.

Ribbon and Lace: Local Craft Store

100% Authentic Printed Twill: 7gypsies

Printed Number Twill: FoofaLa

Bamboo Clip: 7gypsies

Metal Number Stencil: Li'l Davis Designs

Photo Turns: 7gypsies

Mini Brad: Making Memories

Adhesives: UHU Glue Stick; E-6000

Tools: 1/8" Hole Punch by Fiskars

[INSTRUCTIONS]

Cut and fold cardstock to make card. Glue script paper to folded card. Cut and glue word and floral papers to card. Adhere vintage postcard image to front and add bamboo clip with tag sticker. Glue ribbon, lace and twill to card as shown. Adhere sticker word to card and add metal number stencil with E-6000. Punch hole in top and add photo turns with a mini brad to hold in place.

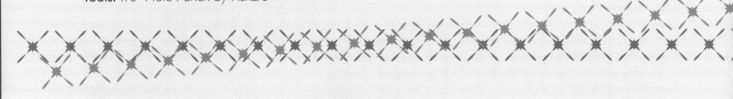

Treasure

ROBEN-MARIE SMITH

[MATERIALS]

Black Cardstock: Local Craft Store

Printed Word Paper: Carolee's Creations

Green Crackle Paper: Bo-Bunny Press

Jet Black StazOn Solvent Ink: Tsukineko

Seashells Sandal Dye Ink: Ranger Industries

"Girl in Hat" Rubber Stamp: Paperbag Studios

Silk Leaf: ARTchix Studio

Silk Flower: Local Craft Store

Ribbon Charms: Making Memories

Mini Brad: Making Memories

Black Metal Floral Washer: American Tag

Adhesives: UHU Glue Stick; Glue Dots International

Other: Sponge

[INSTRUCTIONS]

Cut and fold black cardstock to make card. Cut and glue word paper to card front. Cut pieces of crackle paper and add ribbon charms to strips; glue to card. Stamp "Girl in Hat" with black ink and sponge with Seashell Sandal dye ink. Cut out stamped image and layer to black cardstock and crackle paper; glue to card front. Add mini brad and black metal flower washer to silk flower. Adhere flower and leaf to card with Glue Dots.

Smile, Dream, Love

ROBEN-MARIE SMITH

[MATERIALS]

Cream Cardstock (for card): Local Craft Store:

Floral Paper and Cream Background Paper: K&Company

Vintage Collage Image: Paperbag Studios

Bubble Words: Creative Imaginations

Printed Acetate: 7gypsies

Silk Flower: Local Craft Store

Metal Pewter Frame and Mini Silver Brad: Making Memories

Adhesives: UHU Glue Stick; Glue Dots International

Other: Lace

[INSTRUCTIONS]

Cut and fold cream cardstock into a card. Glue cream background paper to folded card. Adhere printed acetate to the left side of the card with Glue Dots. Tear and glue floral paper to the left edge of the card, and over the acetate, to hide the Glue Dots. Cut another piece of floral paper into a square and glue to card with photo and metal frame on the top. Add a pewter square brad to the center of a silk flower and adhere to card with Glue Dots. Adhere lace with Glue Dots. Peel and stick Bubble Words to bottom right.

Beautiful Tag

AMY WELLENSTEIN

[MATERIALS]

Designer Silver Script: Die Cuts with a View

Tea-Dyed Letters: Renee Plains by Design Originals

Mandolins, Bows, Roses Kraft Paper and Nine Layered Script Paper: Life's Journey by K&Company

Round Black Paper Reinforcement: Local Craft Store

Word on Paper Sticker Strips ("beautiful"): Life's Journey by K&Company

Large Shipping Tag: Local Craft Store or Office Supply

Coffee Archival Dye Inkpad: Ranger Industries

Script Rubber Stamp #JV142G: Limited Edition Rubberstamps

Adhesives: UHU Glue Stick

Other: Clear laminate and color copy of vintage photo

Tools: Sewing machine, black thread and a paper punch (to punch hole in tag)

[INSTRUCTIONS]

1. Use glue stick to layer torn papers to a large shipping tag; flip and trim.

2. Stamp "script" on top left corner using coffee dye ink.

3. Punch the original hole through the top of the tag and adhere a black paper reinforcement over the hole.

4. Use clear laminate technique* to transfer color copy of photo.

5. Layer the transfer on patterned script paper. Adhere the transfer to the center of the tag.

6. Closely stitch several frames around the transfer using black thread and a sewing machine.

*See page 51 for technique instruction

Baby Wish

[MATERIALS]

Black Cardstock (for card): Bazzill

Black and White Floral Cardstock: The Paper Company

Simply Stated Rub-On Transfers (Expressions): Making Memories

Ribbon: Midori

Metal-Rimmed Tag and Antique White Oval Label Holder: Making Memories

Adhesives: Scotch Double-Stick and Foam Tape

Other: Photograph

[INSTRUCTIONS]

1. Cut and fold black cardstock into a card.

2. Cut and press photo to the inside of an oval label holder.

3. Thread wide ribbon through the small holes in the label holder.

4. Cut a panel from black and white floral cardstock to fit on the front of a 4 1/4" × 5 1/2" card.

5. Wrap the ribbon ends to the back of the panel and secure in place with double-stick tape.

6. Secure the label holder to the panel using foam tape.

7. Transfer the word "WISH" to a metal-rimmed tag using rub-ons.

8. Mount the entire panel onto a black card.

TREASURE EACH DAY

[MATERIALS]

Floral Paper: K&Company

Blue Cardstock (for card): Paper Cuts

Pharmacy Label: Stamper's Anonymous

Vintage Postcard Collage Image: Paperbag Studios

Simply Stated Rub-On Words: Making Memories

Ribbon: Local Craft Store

Silk Flowers: Local Craft Store

Metal Label Holder, Alphabet Charms, Decorative Brad and Mini Brad: Making Memories

Adhesives: UHU Glue Stick; Glue Dots International

[INSTRUCTIONS]

Cut and fold dark blue cardstock to make a card. Trim floral paper as shown and glue to front. Adhere vintage postcard image and pharmacy label to card. Cut and fold a small piece of dark blue cardstock; glue to bottom left of card and adhere metal alphabets with Glue Dots. Apply rub-on words to card in top right corner. Add ribbon to label holder and adhere to card over words with Glue Dots. Add brads to silk flowers and glue to card. Tie ribbon in a bow around card.

ROBIN MARIE SMITH

"In childhood, time is kind. A moment is swallowed whole, by senses open and able."

~ Nicoletta Baumeister

SUMMERTIME TAG

AMY WELLENSTEIN

[MATERIALS]

Dictionary Printed Paper: Life's Journey by K&Company

Green Tag: Life's Journey by K&Company

Date and Numbers Rub-On Lettering: Autumn Leaves

Botanical Epoxy Donuts: The Attic Collection by Rebecca Sower/EK Success

Black Sticky Mesh: Making Memories

Small Card Holder: Anima Designs

Brads: Making Memories

Adhesives: Xyron Machine; UHU Glue Stick

Other: Photograph

[INSTRUCTIONS]

1. Adhere an epoxy donut over the hole on the top of the tag.

2. Attach a strip of black sticky mesh across the tag.

3. Use Xyron to adhere a photograph over the mesh.

4. Use glue stick to adhere a piece of dictionary paper to the bottom of the tag.

5. Use rub-ons to transfer the word "SUMMER" to the tag.

6. Use brads to hold a card holder over the word "SUMMER".

Vintage Father's Day Card

PATTI MUMA

[MATERIALS]

Black and Tan Cardstock:
Local Craft Store

Plaid Paper: Paper Patch

Old Measures Paper: K&Company

Typewriter Stickers: Nostalgiques
by Rebecca Sower/EK Success

Scalloped Tags: Hand-Cut by Artist

Sepia Archival Inkpad: Ranger Industries

Aged Clip: 7gypsies

Adhesives: Avery Glue Stick; E-6000

Other: Copy of vintage photo, sponge
for inks, file reference tab, tiny rusted
key and old coin

Tools: Fiskars 12-inch Paper Cutter,
scissors and awl

[INSTRUCTIONS]

Cut and fold black cardstock for card.
Tear plaid paper on side and glue to card.
Mount photo onto black cardstock and
attach file reference tab. Slide computer-
generated text (Hero) into tab. Matte
the photo onto tan cardstock and attach
to front of card. Clip on aged paperclip.

   Cut a piece of Old Measures paper the
length of the card and glue to card's right
side. Sponge scalloped tags with sepia ink
and attach brads. Place letter stickers
onto tags and card as shown.

INSIDE

Cut a small sqaure of black cardstock
(2 1/2" x 2 1/2"). Cut a square of tan
cardstock slightly larger. Matte the black
cardstock onto the tan. Computer-
generate text on standard printer paper.
Tear in square shape and sponge edges
with sepia ink. Glue to center of black
square. Use E-6000 to attach key and
coin. Glue squares onto card.

Nostalgic Collage Squares

MAGGIE CRAWFORD

[MATERIALS]

Patterned Papers: Laura Ashley by K&Company and 7gypsies papers

Vanilla Cardstock (for card): Bazzill

Adhesives: UHU Glue Stick; Judi Kins Diamond Glaze

Other: Button

Tools: Square punch (optional)

[INSTRUCTIONS]

1. Fold vanilla cardstock in half to create card.

2. Punch 25 squares 3/4'' x 3/4'' from scraps of coordinating patterned papers. Glue them to the card, five across and five down until the whole card is covered.

3. Use Diamond Glaze to adhere a button to one of the squares.

Yesterday

MAGGIE CRAWFORD

[MATERIALS]

Vanilla Cardstock (for card): Bazzill

Brown Cardstock: Bazzill

Vellum: Laura Ashley by K&Company

Brown StazOn Solvent Inkpad: Tsukineko

"Yesterday" Rubber Stamp: Local Craft Store

Button: Laura Ashley by K&Company

Adhesives: UHU Glue Stick; Provo Craft Double-Sided Sticky Tape

[INSTRUCTIONS]

1. Fold vanilla cardstock in half to create card.

2. Cut a piece of 4 1/4" x 3 1/2" flower vellum. Tear across the bottom and attach it to the top of the card.

3. Cut brown cardstock to 4 1/4" x 2" and tear across the top. Attach to the bottom of the card, leaving a gap of about 3/4'' between it and the vellum.

4. Attach a piece of binding or ribbon across the brown strip with double-sided sticky tape and stamp "Yesterday" on it.

5. Glue a button to the card between the brown cardstock and vellum.

[MATERIALS]

Pink Cardstock (for card): Bazzill

Text Paper: 7gypsies

Rose Stitching Paper: Sandylion Sticker Designs

"Grow" Transparency: Elements by Daisy D's

Top Boss Clear Pigment Inkpad: Clearsnap

"Beauty Mosaic" Rubber Stamp: Stampotique Originals

Medium Slide Mounts: Local Craft Store

Faux Soldered Word Charm ("Treasures"): Life's Journey by K&Company

Gold Ultra Thick Embossing Enamel (UTEE): Suze Weinberg

Chipboard: Local Craft Store

Adhesives: UHU Glue Stick; Scotch Double-Stick Tape

Other: Butterfly wings cut from decorative gift wrap and a photograph

Treasures

AMY WELLENSTEIN

[INSTRUCTIONS]

1. Layer photo and transparency between several slide mounts to create depth.

2. Line the back slide with pink stitching paper.

3. Cover the front slide with patterned paper.

4. Adhere a faux soldered charm ("Treasures") to the bottom of the slide frame.

5. Super emboss a square of chipboard with gold UTEE. Press "Beauty Mosaic" rubberstamp into hot melted powder; let dry slightly and lift carefully.

Backgammon MAGGIE CRAWFORD

[MATERIALS]

Brown Cardstock (for card): Bazzill

White Cardstock: Bazzill

Ochre, Brown and Dark Brown Inkpads: Marvy Matchables

Rubber Stamps: "Backgammon Man" by River City Rubberworks; "We do not Remember…" by Wordsworth

Adhesives: UHU Glue Stick; Judi Kins Diamond Glaze

Other: Three tiny buttons

[INSTRUCTIONS]

1. Stamp a 5 1/4" x 4" piece of white cardstock all over with words and glue to folded 8 1/2" x 5 1/2" brown card.

2. Cut eight tall triangles from two 4 1/4" x 2 3/4" pieces of brown cardstock. Glue to the white card to resemble a backgammon board.

3. Use brown ink to stamp image of man on a separate piece of white cardstock; stipple brown ink over the image to age it. Glue to a piece of brown cardstock 1/2" larger and then glue to the center of card.

4. Glue three tiny buttons to the image and put a drop of Diamond Glaze on the letters.

MEMORIES
MAGGIE CRAWFORD

[MATERIALS]

Patterned Paper: Legacy Collage by Beth Cote for Design Originals

Scrabble Letters Paper: 7gypsies

Brown Cardstock (for card): Bazzill

Caramel, Terra Cotta and Ginger Adirondack Dye Inkpads: Ranger Industries

Eyelets: Making Memories

Adhesive: UHU Glue Stick

Tools: Tag Punch by Marvy Uchida, hole punch, hammer, eyelet setter; stipple brush, Xacto knife and cutting mat

[INSTRUCTIONS]

1. Fold a piece of 8 1/2" x 5 1/2" brown cardstock in half.

2. Cut a strip of Legacy Collage paper 5" x 3" and tear it down the right-hand side. Using a stipple brush and Adirondack dye inks in Caramel, Terra Cotta and Ginger, stipple ink over the paper to give it an aged look. Glue to the left-hand side of the card.

3. Cut a triangle from the Legacy Collage paper and stipple as before. Attach to the right-hand side of the card.

4. Use Xacto knife to cut two sets of vertical slits, 3/4" high, about one inch from the bottom of the card. Weave a 1/2" x 5 1/2" strip of brown paper through the slits. Secure strip to card with eyelets.

5. Punch two tags from patterned paper with the Marvy punch and attach to the center of the card with eyelets.

Lace Up Card MAGGIE CRAWFORD

[MATERIALS]

Brown Cardstock (for card): Bazzill

White Cardstock: Bazzill

Caramel, Terra Cotta and Ginger Adirondack Dye Inkpads: Ranger Industries

Rubber Stamps: "Letters" by Stamp in the Hand; "Negative Words" and "Italian Script" by Stampers Anonymous; "Music" by Rubbermoon Stamping Company

Eyelets: Making Memories

Adhesive: UHU Glue Stick

Other: Waxed linen thread

Tools: Stipple brushes, 1/4'" hole punch, ruler, hammer, and eyelet setter

[INSTRUCTIONS]

1. Stamp the four different images on 2 3/4" x 2 1/8" white cardstock. Stipple with Adirondack inks so that each is a different shade of brown. Attach to folded 8" x 5" brown cardstock.

2. Punch five pairs of holes down the center of the card, starting 1/2" from the top and spaced at 1" intervals.

3. Put an eyelet in each of the holes and then lace thread through the holes. Tie at the bottom.

Grace
MAGGIE CRAWFORD

[MATERIALS]

Black Linen Paper (for card): Wasau

Music Paper: Penny Black

Brown Cardstock: Bazzill

Scrabble Letters Paper: Limited Edition Rubberstamps

Adhesive: UHU Glue Stick

Other: Embroidery floss and image of woman

Tools: Tag Punch by Marvy Uchida, 1/4''' hole punch and stipple brushes

[INSTRUCTIONS]

1. Tear a 5 1/2'' x 4 1/4'' piece of decorative paper in half diagonally.
   Glue to the left-hand side of folded 8 1/2'' x 5 1/2'' black card.

2. Cut out image of a woman and mount onto a piece of brown cardstock; trim slightly larger than phtograph. Glue to the center of the card.

3. Cut the word "GRACE" from Scrabble tiles and glue above the image.

Three Tags
MAGGIE CRAWFORD

[MATERIALS]

Patterned Paper: Local Craft Store

Brown and Light Brown Cardstock: Bazzill

Woman Images: ARTchix Studio

Ochre, Brown and Dark Brown Inkpads: Marvy Matchables

Goldrush MetaleXtra Inkpad: Colorbox by Clearsnap

Background Image Rubber Stamps: Stampers Anonymous

Adhesives: UHU Glue Stick; foam mounting tape

Other: Embroidery floss

Tools: Tag Punch by Marvy Uchida, 1/4''' hole punch and stipple brushes

[INSTRUCTIONS]

1. Cut a 5 1/2'' x 2'' piece of decorative paper and glue it to the top of folded 8 1/2'' x 5 1/2'' brown cardstock. Stipple some brown ink on the paper.

2. Punch three tags out of light brown card and decorate with stamped images using brown and gold inks. Glue an image to the center of each tag.

3. Punch a small hole in the top of the tag; thread embroidery floss through the hole.

4. Attach tags down the center of the card with foam mounting tape.

"Life is either a daring adventure or nothing at all.
Security is mostly a superstition. It does not exist in nature."
– Helen Keller

Beautiful Baby

AMY WELLENSTEIN

abcdefghijklmnopqrstuvwxy
abcdefghijklmnopqrstuvwxy
abcdefghijklmnopqrstuvwxy

[MATERIALS]

Black Cardstock (for card): Bazzill

Cream Cardstock: Bazzill

Patterned Paper: 7gypsies

Square Tag: Making Memories

Latte Adirondack Dye Inkpad: Ranger Industries

Vintage Sepia and Onyx Black VersaFine Inkpads: Tsukineko

Rubber Stamps: "Happy," "Birthday" and Interactive Cube ("PULL HERE") by Stampotique Originals; Italian Text by Rubber Baby Buggy Bumpers

Black Eyelet: Making Memories

Adhesives: UHU Glue Stick; Scotch Double-Stick Tape

Other: Photograph and page from an old book

Tools: Exacto knife and cutting mat

[INSTRUCTIONS]

1. Create a tall black card with a white inserted "pull-up" strip.

2. Carefully, cut a window in the front of the black card with an exacto knife to fit over strip.

3. Adhere decorative paper around the window on the front of the card.

4. Adhere a photo of a baby to the top half of the pull-up. Embellish with a crown (cut from decorative paper) and a small word (cut from the page of an old book).

5. Stamp Italian text with Latte ink on the bottom half of the pull-up. Stamp "Happy" and "Birthday" over the text stamp using Vintage Sepia ink.

6. Assemble the pull-up card using double-stick tape (keeping the tape clear of the pull-up's path).

7. Set an eyelet at the top of the pull-up.

8. Stamp "PULL HERE" on a square tag using Onyx Black ink. Tie the tag through the eyelet.

Remembering Oprah

JILL HAGLUND

[MATERIALS]

Prefolded Ivory Card: Local Craft Store

"Ledger" Paper: Daisy D's

Letter Stickers: "P,""R,""A" and "H" by: K&Company;

Letter "O": by Li'l Davis Designs

Large Clear Page Pebble: Making Memories

Circle Tag and Shipping Tag: Local Craft Store or Office Supply

Rose Cat's Eye Pigment Inkpad: Colorbox by Clearsnap

Floral and Striped Fabrics: available through Fabric or Craft Store

Metal Disc: Li'l Davis Designs

Adhesives: Yes! Paste; The Ultimate! Glue; Sobo Craft and Fabric Glue

Other: Craft button thread, lace and buttons

Tools: Sewing needle, Fiskars 12-inch Paper Cutter or craft knife and mat

[INSTRUCTIONS]

Paste Ledger paper to pre-folded cardstock as a base. Glue and layer fabrics to paper. Place card between waxed paper and press under the weight of a heavy book; dry flat. Trim all paper from edges of card with paper cutter or craft knife to fit card size exactly. Rub Cat's Eye Rose ink onto both tags. Tie tag with lace. Press vintage photo under Page Pebble, trim and adhere to circle tag. Press "O" into disc and adhere all letters to tag. Sew button with thread and glue to card.

Just Imagine

JILL HAGLUND

"This world is but a canvas to our imagination."
- Henry David Thoreau

[MATERIALS]

Pre-folded Ivory Card: Local Craft Store

Conservatory Stripe Paper: Daisy D's

Music Tissue Paper: 7gypsies

Oval Frame: K&Company

Metal Message ("imagine"): Li'l Davis Designs

Adhesives: Yes! Paste; The Ultimate! Glue; Sobo Craft and Fabric Glue

Other: Small jar of instant coffee, postage stamp, fabric, flower, button and definition of "collage" from dictionary

Tools: Fiskars 12-inch Paper Cutter or craft knife and mat

[INSTRUCTIONS]

Coffee-dye copy of "collage" definition. Paste Conservatory Stripe paper to pre-folded ivory card. Place card between waxed paper and press under the weight of a heavy book; dry flat. Trim to fit card with paper cutter or craft knife. Use fabric glue to layer fabric. Add a small piece of black card stock for a mini collage background. Dry flat.

Collage music tissue, collage definition and postage stamp onto black paper with Yes! Paste. Press photo into small round metal frame. Glue heavier pieces like the frame, metal "imagine" and buttons onto the black card stock with The Ultimate! Glue. With this many little bulky items, I cover with plastic wrap and dry flat once more. The secret to a nice flat card is complete drying in between steps to ensure smoothness. It requires patience at times, but the outcome is worth the effort.

SPREAD cheer

Spread Cheer ROBEN-MARIE SMITH

[MATERIALS]

Ivory Cardstock (for card): Local Craft Store

Papers: Anna Griffin

Sticker Words: Color Oasis Phrases by EK Success

Vintage Collage Image: Paperbag Studios

Lace and ribbon: Local Craft Store

Metallic Green Photo Corners: Canson

Adhesives: UHU Glue Stick; Glue Dots International

Other: Vintage buttons

[INSTRUCTIONS]

Cut and fold ivory paper for card. Cut, layer and glue papers to card as shown. Add photo corners to vintage image and attach to card. Glue lace to left side of photo. Use Glue Dots to adhere buttons. Peel and stick words to card. Cut ribbon and glue to top left corner.

Solitude

ROBEN-MARIE SMITH

[MATERIALS]

Tan Cardstock (for card): Local Craft Store

Floral Paper: Anna Griffin

Vintage Collage Image: Paperbag Studios

Simply Stated Rub-On Words: Making Memories

Walnut Ink: PostModern Design

Pitch Black Adirondack Inkpad: Ranger Industries

Circle Number Rubber Stamp Images: Treasure Cay

Mica Tile: USArtQuest

Adhesives: UHU Glue Stick; Glue Dots International; Judi Kins Diamond Glaze

Other: Vintage postcard, black paper clip, negative film strip, staple, sheet music and button

[INSTRUCTIONS]

Cut and fold tan cardstock into card. Dye sheet music with walnut ink. Tear and glue floral scrapbook paper and sheet music to the card front. Tear and glue old vintage postcard and vintage image to front of card. Using Diamond Glaze, adhere mica tile over picture. Adhere button with Glue Dots. Stamp numbers and swirls to front of card with black dye ink. Add black clip and piece of film negative to top of card. Transfer rub-on word to card front.

REMEMBER

Father

JANUARY 1969

HAPPY BIRTHDAY

LOVE (lŭv), n. [...] S. lufe, lufu.]
Devotion or attachment to another,
esp., to one of the opposite sex; affection. 2. Courtship. 3. Object of
affection. 4. Benevolence; kindness.
[...] [-ED; -ING.] [A.S ...

oldtimer

Father

AMY WELLENSTEIN

[MATERIALS]

Black Cardstock (for card): Bazzill

Rub-On Lettering (Dates and Numbers): Autumn Leaves

Simply Stated Rub-On Letters ("Providence," Small White): Making Memories

Metal Art Alphabet Discs: Life's Journey by K&Company

Adhesives: The Ultimate! Glue; UHU Glue Stick

Other: Photograph

[INSTRUCTIONS]

1. Adhere a photo to a black card.

2. Use white rub-on letters to transfer the word "Father" to the photo.

3. Use small white rub-on letters to transfer the date to the black card below the photo.

4. Spell out "REMEMBER" with metal alphabet discs. Glue in place using The Ultimate! Glue.

old timer

AMY WELLENSTEIN

[MATERIALS]

Black File Folio: FoofaLa

Text: 7gypsies

Black Cardstock: Bazzill

Love Stickers, Domed Random Alphabet Reversed, Black Label Words and Sayings: Life's Journey by K&Company

Old Alphabet: Karen Foster

Adhesives: UHU Glue Stick; Scotch Double-Stick Tape

Other: Photograph

[INSTRUCTIONS]

1. Tear a strip of text paper and use glue stick to attach it to the front of a black file folio.

2. Layer a photograph on black cardstock; mount onto the folio.

3. Embellish the folio with alphabet and phrase stickers.

Long Brown Card with Tags

AMY WELLENSTEIN

[MATERIALS]

Arithmetique Red Paper and Carte Postale Cardstock Stickers: 7gypsies

Antique Ruler Sticker: Nostalgiques by Rebecca Sower/EK Success

White Text Weight Paper: Local Office Supply

Brown Cardstock (for card): Bazzill

Small Shipping Tags: Local Craft Store or Office Supply

Rust Adirondack Dye Inkpad: Ranger Industries

Coffee and Sepia Archival Dye Inkpads: Ranger Industries

Rubber Stamps: Italian Text by Rubber Baby Buggy Bumpers; "Dear Elizabeth" and "Antique Border" by Stampotique Originals

Copper Mesh: American Art Clay Company, Inc.

Adhesives: The Ultimate! Glue; UHU Glue Stick; Scotch Double-Stick Tape

Tools: Small and medium heart punches by EK Success, exacto knife and mat

[INSTRUCTIONS]

1. Remove strings from all tags; save one string for the second tag.

2. For the first tag, stamp antique border in sepia ink on the lower left corner of the tag. Adhere a section of antique ruler sticker across the middle. Punch a medium heart from red paper and adhere it to the tag using glue stick.

3. For the second tag, stamp "Dear Elizabeth" on a piece of white text weight paper. Fold the paper and age with Coffee ink. Punch a small heart from red paper and adhere it to the "letter" with glue stick. Tie a string from one of the tags around the letter and adhere it to the tag.

4. For the third tag, punch a medium-sized heart from a piece of red paper. Glue the negative heart onto a tag using glue stick.

5. For the fourth tag, use an exacto knife to cut an "L" stencil from the tag. Stamp "Italian Text" using Rust ink on the right side of the tag. Punch a small heart from copper mesh and glue it to the tag.

6. For the fifth tag, adhere a small postcard sticker to the tag; trim if needed.

7. Use double-stick tape to attach all five tags to a long brown card.

Tall Girl Holding Heart AMY WELLENSTEIN

[MATERIALS]

Red Patterned Paper: Daisy D's

Dictionary Printed Vellum: Life's Journey by K&Company

Ivory Cardstock (for card): Bazzill

Clearly Yours Hearts and Stars Stickers ("Soul Heart"): Life's Journey by K&Company

Sepia Archival Dye Inkpad: Ranger Industries

Adhesives: UHU Glue Stick; Scotch Double-Stick Tape

Other: Photographs and scrap of text paper

[INSTRUCTIONS]

1. Use ivory cardstock to create a tall card.

2. Fold a piece of patterned vellum over the card. Secure with a small strip of double-stick tape on the front side.

3. Use photographs, red patterned paper and a scrap of text paper (Crown) to create a mini collage.

4. Adhere the collage to the front of the card.

5. Embellish the collage with a dimensional heart sticker.

Winged Beauty

AMY WELLENSTEIN

[MATERIALS]

Plum Cardstock (for card): Magenta

Black Cardstock: Bazzill

Butterfly Collage Paper: K&Company

Butterfly Frame Stickers: Grand Adhesions by K&Company

Adhesives: UHU Glue Stick; Scotch Double-Stick Tape

Other: Photograph and wings from giftwrap

[INSTRUCTIONS]

1. Adhere a photograph with added wings to cardstock (for stability) and trim out.

2. Use double-stick tape to tape the photo to a decorative sticker frame.

3. Glue patterned paper to a panel of black cardstock. Mount the panel on a plum-colored card.

4. Adhere the sticker frame to the card.

Pixie AMY WELLENSTEIN

[MATERIALS]

Green Patterned Paper: Sweetwater

Layered Script Paper (used for Crown and Wings), Ledger Printed Paper, Butterfly Collage Paper: Life's Life's Journey by K&Company

Cream Cardstock (for card): Bazzill

"Twill Tape Thoughts" Strips, "ABCs" Labels and "Itty Bitty Love" Tags: Real Life Cardstock Stickers by Pebbles, Inc.

Sepia Archival Dye Inkpad: Ranger Industries

Adhesive: UHU Glue Stick

Other: Color copy of photograph

[INSTRUCTIONS]

1. Sponge the edges of a piece of green patterned paper with sepia ink.

2. Adhere a twill tape sticker ("faith") across the bottom; trim as needed.

3. Use glue stick to adhere a photograph to the paper. Embellish with small wings and a crown (cut from patterned paper).

4. Adhere a small tag sticker near the hand of the photo, to give the appearance of holding the tag.

5. Spell out "PIXIE" with alphabet stickers across the top.

6. Layer the green patterned paper on cream ledger paper. Sponge the edges with sepia ink.

7. Layer onto purple patterned paper and then mount on a cream card.

"The pursuit of truth and beauty is a sphere of activity in which we are permitted to remain children all our lives" ~ Albert Einstein

Oriental Travel Tag

AMY WELLENSTEIN

[MATERIALS]

Green Script Paper: Life's Journey by K&Company

Clearly Yours Round Stamp Dimensional Alphabet Stickers: Life's Journey by K&Company

Large Shipping Tag: Local Craft Store or Office Supply

Small Black Paper Disc: Lost Art Treasures by American Tag

"Travel" Transparency: Daisy D's Elements

Ribbon: ARTchix Studio

Adhesives: Xyron Machine; UHU Glue Stick

Other: Photograph

[INSTRUCTIONS]

1. Cover a large shipping tag with patterned paper.

2. Adhere a black disc over the hole on the tag.

3. Tie a decorative ribbon through the hole.

4. Adhere a photograph to the tag.

5. Use Xyron to adhere a strip of transparency on the lower left side of the tag, partially overlapping the photo.

6. Use K&Company's dimensional alphabet stickers to spell out "HELLO" along the right side of the tag.

LA BEAUTÉ NATURELLE

Une peau saine et un joli teint dépend
du renouvellement régulier des déchets epi
les pores sont obstrués par des déchets epi
dermiques ou autres impuretés, la peau perd
sa vitalité. Il convient donc de dégager les
pores par de fréquents lavages avec un savon
pur, tel que le Savon Cadum dont la mousse
abondante enlève toutes impuretés et stimule
les fonctions naturelles des pores

Vintage Paris PATTI MUMA

[MATERIALS]

Old Measures and Buttons Paper: K&Company

Musique, Advertisme and Script Tissue Papers: 7gypsies

Manila Folder, Coin Envelope and Black Cardstock: Local Craft Store

Vintage Photo: Lost Art Treasures

Tri-Fold Tag and Scalloped Tag: Hand-Cut by Artist

Transparency Eiffel Tower and Ticket Stubs from Paris Collage Sheet: ARTchix Studio

Terra Cotta, Ochre and Brown Dye Inkpads: Marvy Matchables

Leaf Green Inkpad: Ancient Page by Clearsnap

Jet Black StazOn Solvent Inkpad: Tsukineko

Walnut Ink Crystals: Postmodern Design

Clear Embossing Powder: Ranger Industries

Rubber Stamp Images: Stampin' Up!

Spiral Clip, Eiffel Tower Charm and Brads: Local Craft Store

Adhesives: Avery Glue Stick; Super Bond Glue

Other: Fibers and Scrabble tile letters

Tools: Scissors, spray bottle, Fiskars 12-inch Paper Cutter, eyelet setter, hammer, awl, small circle paper punch and heat gun

[INSTRUCTIONS]

Open manila folder, spray with walnut ink crystals dissolved in distilled water. When dry, use a standard-size tag as template and trace three in a row, making sure they touch (think paper dolls!). Cut out around the outside of tags. Score and fold in accordion fashion. Punch hole on top of each panel using standard-size paper punch.

For the first panel, tear Musique and Button paper, collage on half of panel. Trim panel with Old Measures paper. Use black cardstock to matt the vintage photo, repeat with a section cut from Advertisme paper. Adhere both to tag.

For the second panel, tear a piece of Script tissue paper and glue onto panel. Apply various inkpads directly to the tag to give an aged effect (on the seamed side and flap of the envelope). Place envelope on the center panel. Stamp the scalloped tag in black and emboss. Stamp opposite side of tag and collage with scrap paper. Attach to flap of envelope with a brad. Place spiral clip on bottom of tag. Flip tag up to open envelope, place ticket stubs in envelope.

For the third panel, cut the Eiffel Tower from transparency and attach with brads. Place "Paris" scrabble tiles along bottom with super bond glue.

Thread fibers and ribbons through the top of each panel. Tie the Eiffel Tower charm onto the ribbons of the first panel.

Woman MAGGIE CRAWFORD

[MATERIALS]

Vanilla Cardstock: Bazzill

Brown Cardstock (for card): Bazzill

Medium Weight Vellum: Local Craft Store

Brown StazOn Solvent Inkpad: Tsukineko

Purple, Green and Yellow Inkpads: Marvy
Matchables

Rubber Stamps: Words by My Sentiments
Exactly; Woman by Hero Arts

Adhesive: UHU Glue Stick

Tools: Stipple brushes

[INSTRUCTIONS]

1. Fold brown cardstock in half to create card.
2. Stamp words on a 5" x 1" piece of vanilla cardstock and attach to the left-hand side of the card.
3. Stamp image of woman on vanilla cardstock; color with stipple brushes and Marvy inks.
4. Make a pocket out of clear vellum by folding a 7" x 3" piece of vellum in thirds. Glue along the bottom of the pocket to hold it together, then tear diagonally across the front so that the image is half covered.
5. Put the woman image in the pocket and attach it to 3" x 2" vanilla cardstock, then layer onto 3 1/4" x 2 1/4" brown cardstock. Attach this to the center of the card.

Times to Remember

MAGGIE CRAWFORD

[MATERIALS]

Patterned Paper and Vellum: Laura Ashley by
K&Company

Brown Cardstock: Bazzill

Cream Cardstock (for card): Bazzill

Magenta Inkpad: Marvy Matchables

"Times to Remember" Rubber Stamp:
Paper Parachute

Adhesive: UHU Glue stick

Tools: Oval Punch by EK Success; Scalloped
Oval Punch by Marvy Uchida; Lace Pattern
Punch by Fiskars

[INSTRUCTIONS]

1. Fold brown cardstock in half to create card.
2. Cut brown vellum 5 1/2" x 4" and attach to the front of the card, about 1" from the bottom of the card. Fold excess over the top of the card and glue to the back.
3. Punch the lace border from two 5 1/2" x 3/4" strips of cream card. Attach one border to the bottom of the card and the second to a 5 1/2" x 3/4" strip of brown cardstock. Attach brown strip just above the first border.
4. Punch scallop out of flower paper and oval out of cream paper.
5. Use Majenta ink to stamp "Times to Remember" on cream card stock. Adhere to two layered ovals. Attach to center of card.

Vintage Strip

MAGGIE CRAWFORD

[MATERIALS]

Brown Cardstock (for card): Bazzill

Pink Cardstock: Bazzil

Vellum: Laura Ashley by K&Company

Round Vellum Tags: Local Craft Store

Brown Inkpad: Marvy Matchables

"Vintage" Rubber Stamp: Local Craft Store

Adhesives: UHU Glue Stick;
Scotch foam mounting tape

[INSTRUCTIONS]

1. Fold brown cardstock in half to create card.
2. Cut flower vellum 4 1/4" x 2" and glue to the left-hand side of the card.
3. Stamp the word "Vintage" on a strip of pink card and glue next to the vellum.
4. Cut two circles out of the vellum to fit inside the vellum tags and attach to the right-hand side of the tag with foam mounting tape.

Sisters Love

JILL HAGLUND

[MATERIALS]

Black Cardstock: Local Craft Store

Red Script Paper: 7gypsies

Marbled Paper: Angy's Dreams

Script Paper: Vintage Charmings

Sticker Letters "SISTERS": K&Company

"Dream Compass" Printed Acetate: Life's Journey by K&Company

"Grow" Transparency: Daisy D's Elements

Moss Green and Terra Cotta Cat's Eye Pigment Inkpads: Colorbox by Clearsnap

Small Pewter "dream" Plate: "Charmed Words" by: Making Memories

Adhesives: Yes! Paste; The Ultimate! Glue; Art Accentz Tape by Provo Craft (to adhere transparency)

Other: Buttons, craft button thread and vintage photograph

Tools: Paper cutter and sewing needle

[INSTRUCTIONS]

1. Cut and fold a card from black cardstack.

2. Use a paper cutter to cut papers shown; each slightly smaller than the previous one, to create a matted, layered panel of various sized papers. Layer in this order: red script paper, black cardstock, white cardstock, "Dream Compass" Printed Acetate (use Art Accentz Tape for adhering acetate) and marbled paper.

3. Paste panel to black card, using Yes! Paste.

4. Tear edges of white script paper and rub gently with Cat's Eye inkpads; adhere to card. Add photo. Flatten and dry.

5. Sew thread in buttonholes. Add buttons, "Sisters" sticker and "dream" pewter piece to card.

6. Cut "Grow" transparency and add it to bottom of card with a touch of double-sided Art Accentz Tape.

Trust

ROBEN-MARIE SMITH

[MATERIALS]

Red Diamond and Black Script Papers: 7gypsies

Ivory Paper with Text: Creative Imaginations

Green Paper: Karen Foster Designs

Black Cardstock (for card): Paper Cuts

Jet Black StazOn Solvent Inkpad: Tsukineko

"Prepared to See" Rubber Stamp: Paperbag Studios

Black Beads: Local Craft Store

Black Photo Corners: Canson

"Trust" Charm and Metal Rod: K&Company

Adhesives: UHU Glue Stick; Glue Dots International

[INSTRUCTIONS]

Cut, tear and glue red paper and black script paper to front of folded black card. Stamp "Prepared to See" on ivory paper with black dye ink and mount onto green paper with black photo corners; glue to card. Use Glue Dots to adhere black beads, "trust" charm and metal rod to card.

Butterfly Belle

AMY WELLENSTEIN

[MATERIALS]

Black Cardstock (for card): Bazzill

Cream Script Paper: 7gypsies

Brown Mesh (Maruyama): Magenta

Dictionary Entry ("belle"): FoofaLa

Laminate Film: Local Office Supply

Cameo Pin: 7gypsies

Adhesives: UHU Glue Stick; Scotch Double-Stick Tape

Other: Butterfly wings cut from decorative gift wrap, photograph and page from an old book

[INSTRUCTIONS]

1. Use a piece of laminating film to create a clear laminate transfer of a baby with butterfly wings.*

2. Line the transfer with cream script paper.

3. Layer the transfer on black cardstock and brown mesh.

4. Poke two small holes near the baby's hand and insert a cameo pin.

5. Mount the layered transfer on a black card.

6. Create a small black crown from cardstock and adhere it to the photo.

7. Cut a small number from an old book and adhere it to the crown.

8. Insert a small dictionary entry in the end of the cameo pin.

CLEAR LAMINATE TRANSFER: Adhere laminate onto color copy; smooth and burnish with spoon or bone folder. Soak laminate in water and remove all paper by rubbing with your fingers. What is left is a "clear laminate transfer" of your image. It is much thicker and easier to work with then a packing tape tranfer.

Butterfly Boy **AMY WELLENSTEIN**

[MATERIALS]

Script & Buttons Paper: K&Company

Ivory Cardstock (for card): Bazzill

Pinebough (Pinecone) Paper: Daisy D's

"Love" Bits and Pieces (Heart): Real Life Cardstock Stickers: by Pebbles, Inc.

Wooden Ruler Stickers: Nostalgiques by Rebecca Sower/EK Success

Sepia Archival Dye Inkpad: Ranger Industries

Rectangle Zipper Pulls: Expressions by All My Memories

Adhesives: UHU Glue Stick; Scotch Double-Stick Tape

Other: Photos and various papers

[INSTRUCTIONS]

1. Use photographs, stickers and artists collect of papers to create a mini collage on a panel of script patterned paper.

2. Sponge ink on the edges of the panel and around the image.

3. Layer the panel on a piece of brown patterned paper.

4. Mount the layered panel onto an ivory card.

5. Embellish the collage with a metal tag.

Mariposa **AMY WELLENSTEIN**

[MATERIALS]

Yellow Cardstock (for card): Local Craft Store

Burgundy Floral Paper: Laura Ashley by K&Company

Antique Ruler Paper: Limited Edition Rubberstamps

Self-Stick Alphabet Stickers: HyKo Products Co.

Sepia Archival Dye Inkpad: Ranger Industries

Adhesive: UHU Glue Stick

Other: Color copy of photograph, page from an old book and newsprint paper

[INSTRUCTIONS]

1. Sponge the edges and surface of a page from an old book with sepia ink.

2. Use a photograph and page from old book or newsprint to create a miniature collage.

3. Adhere the collage to the page using glue stick.

4. Adhere an antique ruler to the bottom of the collage.

5. Use small alphabet stickers to spell out "MARIPOSA" across the bottom.

6. Layer the collage onto burgundy floral paper.

7. Mount on a yellow card.

Time to Get Together
PATTI MUMA

[MATERIALS]

Script and Brown Striped Paper: K&Company

Black, Brown Cardstock: Local Craft Store

Plum Cardstock (for card): Local Craft Store

Adhesive-Backed Letters: Real Life Cardstock Stickers by Pebbles, Inc.

Button Stickers: Life's Journey by K&Company

Sepia Archival Dye Inkpad: Ranger Industries

Metal Charm ("dream"): Local Craft Store

Adhesives: Glue Stick; Photo Splits by Pioneer

Other: Vintage photograph

Tools: Fiskars 12-inch Paper Cutter, deckle scissors, fine-grade sandpaper, ruler and sponge

[INSTRUCTIONS]

Cut plum cardstock to desired size and fold into a card. Cut script background paper to fit card front and sponge edges with sepia ink. Cut brown striped paper as a side border then sand edges lightly to age. Glue brown striped paper to script paper with glue stick; press to smooth. Adhere both panels to card.

Print desired photograph onto standard computer paper. Using ruler, tear paper and sand edges lightly, sponge with sepia ink. Layer photo onto dark brown cardstock, then black cardstock. Trim with a deckle edge scissors and glue to card. Add letter stickers to top of card to spell "time." Add button stickers along side of card.

Collections & Memoirs
AMY WELLENSTEIN

[MATERIALS]

Red Cardstock (for card): Bazzill

Cream Cardstock: Bazzill

Red Script Paper and Cream Script Paper: 7gypsies

Dictionary Printed Paper: Life's Journey by K&Company

Grand Adhesions Puzzle Pieces: Life's Journey by K&Company

Laminate Film: Local Office Supply

Sepia Archival Dye Inkpad: Ranger Industries

Rubber Stamps: "Memoirs" and "Collections" by Stampotique Originals

Vintage Safety Pin: 7gypsies

Metal Messages ("Legacy"): Li'l Davis Designs

Small Frame: Life's Journey by K&Company

Adhesives: Thu Ultimate! Glue; UHU Glue Stick; Scotch Double-Stick Tape

Other: Photographs and small glassine envelopes

Tools: Sewing machine

[INSTRUCTIONS]

1. Use a piece of laminating film to create a clear laminate transfer of an old family photo.*

2. Line the transfer with cream script paper.

3. Sew the transfer to a square of red script paper.

4. Layer the red paper on yellow patterned paper, then mount onto a red card.

5. Embellish the card with stickers, metal objects and glassine envelopes.

6. Stamp "Collections" and "Memoirs" on small strips of cream script paper. Put strips into the glassine envelopes and tuck into card embellishments.

*See page 51 for technique instruction.

Numbers Collection

ROBEN-MARIE SMITH

[MATERIALS]

Numbers Paper: 7gypsies

Brown Cardstock (for card): Paper Cuts

Black Numbers Paper: Li'l Davis Designs

Postcard Paper: K&Company

Vintage Collage Image: Paperbag Studios

Black Fine Point Marker: Local Office Supply

Small Jewelry Tags: Local Office Supply

Printed Twill: 7gypsies

Gold Clip and Gold Buckle: 7gypsies

Safety Pin: Making Memories

Adhesives: UHU Glue Stick; Glue Dots International

Other: Vintage buttons, fabric and round numbers

[INSTRUCTIONS]

Cut cardstock and fold to make card. Cut and glue paper to fit front of card. Randomly glue number papers to card. Cut out man image and adhere to card. Attach safety pin to twill and glue to card. Using gold clip, attach buckle to top of card, adding tags and fabric piece. Glue round numbers to tags. Press button to front of man image with Glue Dot.

New Arrival

JILL HAGLUND

[MATERIALS]

Script Papers and Jardin Floral:
K&Company

Pre-folded Black Card:
Local Craft Store

"ABC's" Stickers: Real Life
Cardstock Stickers by Pebbles, Inc.

"Moments" Sticker by:
Li'l Davis Designs

**"Daughter" Transparency and
Daughter Definition:**
Elements Collection by Daisy D's

Metal Photo Corners:
K&Company

Metal Oval Disc:
Li'l Davis Designs

Adhesives: Yes! Paste;
The Ultimate! Glue;
Art Accentz Tape by Provo Craft

Tools: Fiskars 12-inch Paper
Cutter

[INSTRUCTIONS]

Cut and paste floral paper to black
card. Add torn script paper, trimmed
photo and adhesive letters. Press
under weight to dry flat. Adhere
metal photo corners. Press
"Moments" into metal oval disc and
glue to photo. Add transparencies
with a touch of Art Accentz Tape.

"Write it on your heart that every day is the best day in the year."
~ Ralph Waldo Emerson

Dreamer
ROBEN-MARIE SMITH

[MATERIALS]

Papers: 7gypsies

Black Cardstock (for card): Paper Cuts

Rub-On Words: Making Memories

Sticker Label: Li'l Davis Designs

Butterfly Image: Dover Clipart

Ribbon: Offray

Printed Slide Mount: Creative Imaginations

Black Nail Head: 7gypsies

Adhesives: UHU Glue Stick; Glue Dots International

Other: Photograph

Tools: Small Star Punch by Marvy Uchida

[INSTRUCTIONS]

Cut, tear and glue paper to fit front of folded black card. Cut out child image from photograph and glue to card. Attach label to card and add rub-on word to front. Cut out butterfly image and attach to card. Glue ribbon horizontally across the bottom of card and attach nail head with Glue Dot. Place vintage image into slide mount and adhere to card front. Using star punch, create three stars and glue to card front as shown.

[MATERIALS]

Ledger Pad: Making Memories

Pink Floral Paper: Daisy D's

Cream Cardstock (for card): Bazzill

Brown Cardstock: Bazzill

Wooden Ruler Sticker: Nostalgiques by Rebecca Sower/ EK Success

Ransom Alpha/Number Stickers (Number "6"): Real Life Cardstock Stickers by Pebbles, Inc.

Clearly Yours Domed Random Alphabet Reversed Stickers (Number "4"): Life's Journey by K&Company

Sepia Archival Dye Inkpad: Ranger Industries

Onyx Black VersaFine Inkpad: Tsukineko

"Studio Copy" Rubber Stamp: Raindrops on Roses

Adhesive : UHU Glue Stick

Other: Color copy of photograph and scrap of text paper

BOY ON RULER

AMY WELLENSTEIN

[INSTRUCTIONS]

1. Sponge the edges and surface of a piece of ledger paper with sepia ink.

2. Adhere a wooden ruler sticker across the bottom; trim as needed.

3. Use glue stick to adhere a photograph to the paper. Embellish with a small crown (cut from text paper).

4. Adhere a small domed number sticker ("4") to the hat. Adhere a number sticker ("6") to the paper next to the photo.

5. Stamp the "COPY" portion of the "STUDIO COPY" stamp on the lower right corner using black ink.

6. Layer the green patterned paper onto pink floral paper.

7. Layer on brown cardstock and then mount on a cream card.

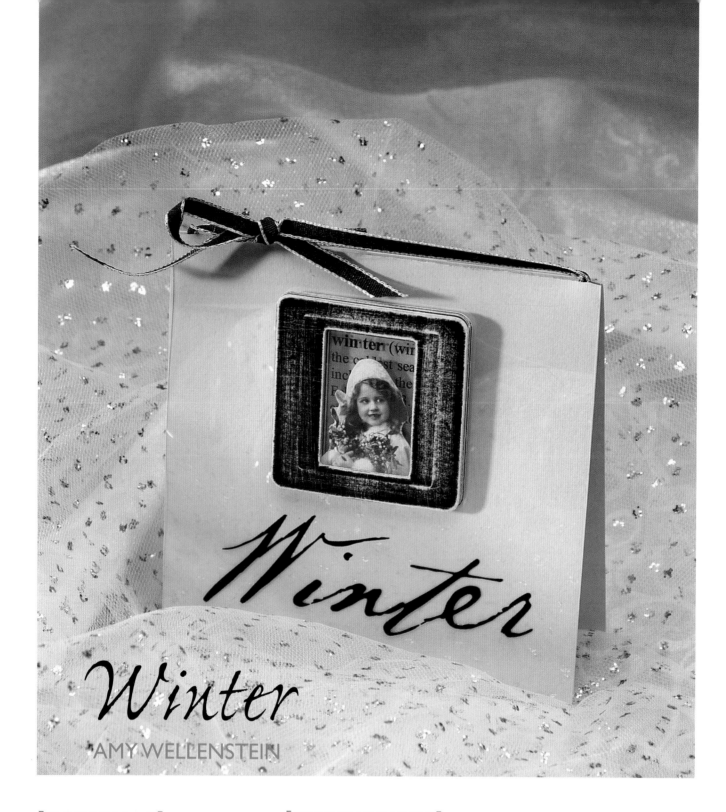

Winter

AMY WELLENSTEIN

[MATERIALS]

Pink and Light Green Cardstock: Bazzill

"Winter" Transparency: Daisy D's Elements

Image: ARTchix Studio

Adhesive: Scotch Double-Stick Tape

Other: Black slide mounts, ribbon and sandpaper

[INSTRUCTIONS]

1. Layer a photo and transparency between several slide mounts to create depth.

2. Line the back slide mount with light green paper.

3. Sand the front of a black slide mount to create a distressed appearance.

4. Attach the sanded slide mount to the front of the other mounts.

5. Adhere "Winter" Transparency to the front of a pink card.

6. Use double-stick tape to adhere the slide mount frame to the front of the card.

7. Tie a ribbon with a bow across the top of the card.

Awake to the Flowers
ROBEN-MARIE SMITH

[MATERIALS]

Black Script and Word Papers: 7gypsies

Number Paper: Daisy D's

Brown Cardstock (for card): Paper Cuts

Vintage Collage Image: Paperbag Studios

White Acrylic Paint: Delta

Black Crayola Crayon: Local Craft Store

Grand Adhesions Flowers: K&Company

Silver Drawer Pull: 7gypsies

Metal Brad: Making Memories

White Heart: DCC

Adhesives: UHU Glue Stick; Glue Dots International

Other: Vintage buttons and old book page

Tools: Paintbrush

[INSTRUCTIONS]

Using a dry bristle brush, sparingly apply ivory acrylic paint to the front of a folded brown card. Tear and glue papers and old book page to card front. Glue vintage image to card and scribble around edges with black crayon. Adhere buttons, brad, handle and white heart to card with Glue Dots.

Girl with Twelve on Heart

AMY WELLENSTEIN

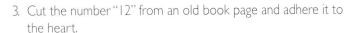

[MATERIALS]

Green Cardstock (for card): Bazzill

Red Cardstock: Bazzill

Bordeaux (Crown): 7gypsies

Duffel Bag Paper: Everafter Scrapbook Company

Stitched Letter Paper: Sweetwater

Red Floral Paper: Anna Griffin

"Itty Bitty Love" Tags:
Real Life Cardstock Stickers by Pebbles, Inc.

Sepia Archival Dye Inkpad: Ranger Industries

Adhesives: UHU Glue Stick

Other: Color copy of photograph and page
from an old book

[INSTRUCTIONS]

1. Sponge the edges and surface
   of a page from an old book
   with sepia ink.

2. Use glue stick to adhere a cutout
   photograph to the paper. Embellish with a
   small crown (cut from patterned paper)
   and a red heart cut from cardstock.

3. Cut the number "12" from an old book page and adhere it to
   the heart.

4. Adhere a small tag sticker near the hand of the photo (to give
   the appearance of holding the tag).

5. Layer the text paper onto green Duffel Bag paper.

6. Layer both onto stiched letter paper, then to red floral paper.

7. Mount all on a green card.

Remember

AMY WELLENSTEIN

[MATERIALS]

Green Cardstock (for card): Bazzill

Brown Cardstock: Bazzill

Layered Script Paper and Gazette Paper:
Life's Journey by K&Company

Black Label Embossed "REMEMBER" Stickers:
Life's Journey by K&Company

Coffee Archival Dye Inkpad: Ranger Industries

"Antique Border" Rubber Stamp:
by Stampotique Originals

Small Alpha Charm: Making Memories

Metal Art Tag: Life's Journey by K&Company

Safety Pin: Local Craft Store

Adhesives: The Ultimate! Glue;
Scotch Double-Stick Tape

Other: Color copy of vintage photo and clear laminate

[INSTRUCTIONS]

1. Use clear laminate technique to transfer color copy of vintage
   photo.*

2. Layer transfer on patterned script paper; trim to size.

3. Layer transfer on brown cardstock.

4. Stamp antique border on green card using dye-based ink.

5. Adhere photo to card using double-stick tape.

6. Cut a small crown from a scrap of paper and paste to photo.

7. Glue a small alpha charm on the crown.

8. Use a small safety pin to attach "dream" charm to the top edge
   of card.

   * See page 51 for technique instruction.

REMEMBER

journey

[MATERIALS]

Musique Tissue Paper and Mesurement Paper: 7gypsies

Manila Folder and Coin Envelope: Local Office Supply

Typewritter Letters: Nostalgiques by Rebecca Sower/EK Success

Mid-Size Tag: Rusty Pickle

Large Round Metal-Rimmed Tag: Local Office Supply

"Journey" Bubble Phrase Sticker: Li'l Davis Designs

Sepia Archival Inkpad: Ranger Industries

Light Brown Inkpad: Ancient Page by Clearsnap

Brown, Terra Cotta and Ochre Inkpads: Marvy Matchables

Walnut Ink Crystals: Postmodern Design

Little Typewriter Letters Rubber Stamps: Hero Arts

Metal Oval Frames: Li'l Davis Designs

Brads: Local Craft Store

Eyelets: Making Memories

Adhesives: Glue Stick and Super Bond Glue

Other: Vintage photo trimmed to silhouette, a piece of exposed film (i.e., an old negative), tri-fold and small scalloped tags (hand-cut by artist), and fibers

Tools: Scissors, Fiskars 12-inch Paper Cutter, spray bottle, eyelet setter, hammer, awl and small circle paper punch

"*Don't marry the person you think you can live with; marry only the individual you think you can't live without.*"
- Dr. James C. Dobson

Vintage Wedding
PATTI MUMA

[INSTRUCTIONS]

Open manila folder, spray with walnut ink crystals dissolved in water. When dry, use a standard-size tag as template and trace three in a row, making sure they touch (think paper dolls!). Cut out around the outside of tags. Score and fold in accordion fashion. Punch hole on top of each panel using standard-size paper punch.

For the first panel, place vintage photo using glue stick. For the small tag, using a paper punch, punch small numbers from Mesurement paper and adhere to tag with glue stick. Attach this small tag with a brad.

For the center panel, tear a piece of Musique tissue and adhere to tag with glue stick. Add typewriter stickers. Computer-generate text, tear and age edges with ink. (Variation: CAREFULLY burn edges with a match over kitchen sink.) Attach text to large circle tag and attach large tag to panel with brad. Press Bubble Phrase sticker on metal oval frame, glue to panel.

For the third panel, age a coin envelope with walnut ink and allow to dry. Stamp phrase of choice with letter stamps. Fold filmstrip lengthwise in half. Place over the bottom edge of envelope; use super bond glue to adhere. Then using eyelet setter, attach eyelets at bottom of envelope. Attach envelope, place tag inside envelope.

Add fibers to each of the panels.

SLIDE OUT

AMY WELLENSTEIN

[MATERIALS]

**Black Cardstock
(outer pocket):** Bazzill

Black Cardstock:
Local Craft Store

Brown Patterned Paper:
7gypsies

**Dictionary Printed
Paper:** Life's Journey
by K&Company

**Forget Me Not Collage
(Leaf Friendship Sticker):**
Life's Journey by
K&Company

Magazine Font Stickers:
Rusty Pickle

Index Tab:
Local Office Supply

**Onyx Black VersaFine
Inkpad:** Tsukineko

Rubber Stamps:
Interactive Cube
("Slide Out") and
"Snap Border" by
Stampotique Originals

Adhesives:
UHU Glue Stick; Scotch
Double-Stick Tape

Other: Photograph and
butterfly wings cut from
decorative gift wrap

[INSTRUCTIONS]

1. Use glue stick to adhere photo to an index tab. Embellish photo with wings, a hat and a number sticker.

2. Stamp "Slide Out" on the tab and snap border down the right side.

3. Fold black cardstock to create a pocket card. Use double-stick tape to secure the top and bottom edges.

4. Tear the edge of a piece of brown patterned paper.

5. Use glue stick to adhere brown patterned paper to the front of the card.

6. Embellish the front of the card with a round sticker.

Home Sweet Home

AMY WELLENSTEIN

[MATERIALS]

Cream Cardstock: Bazzill

Hearts and Stars: Life's Journey by K&Company

Mat Board: Local Craft Store

Sepia and Butterscotch Adirondack Dye Inkpad: Ranger Industries

Onyx Black VersaFine Inkpad: Tsukineko

Platinum Ultra Thick Embossing Enamel: Suze Weinberg

Rubber Stamps: "Dear Elizabeth," "Lace Border," "Tall Alphabet," "Stencil Background" and "Hook and Eye Border" by Stampotique Originals

Small Alpha Charms: Making Memories

Rectangle Frames: Metal Memorabilia by Li'l Davis Designs

Small Handle: 7gypsies

Adhesives: UHU Glue Stick; Scotch Double-Stick Tape

Other: Photograph and ledger transparency

[INSTRUCTIONS]

1. Trim mat board into two house-shaped covers.

2. Sponge Butterscotch and Sepia inks on the covers.

3. Stamp covers with "Dear Elizabeth" and "Lace Border" using Onyx Black ink.

4. Create a small frame for the front cover using mat board.

5. Super emboss the "Stencil Background Stamp" on the frame using platinum embossing enamel.

6. Line the frame with a small piece of printed transparency.

7. Glue alpha charms into rectangle frames to spell the word "HOME." Glue the title to the front cover.

8. Adhere a small heart sticker above the title.

9. Attach a handle to the right side of the front cover.

[INSTRUCTIONS] for inside

10. Create a house-shaped card from cream cardstock to fit inside the covers.

11. Stamp "Hook and Eye Border" on the left side of the card. Stamp "SWEET HOME" on the left side of the card.

12. Glue a small photo to the left side of the card.

13. Adhere the covers to the card; trim out the window on the front cover.

14. Adhere a heart-shaped sticker to the inside of the card above the window.

15. Use double-stick tape to adhere the frame to the front cover.

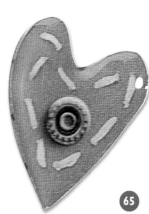

Cherish

ROBEN-MARIE SMITH

[MATERIALS]

Olive Cardstock (for card): Local Craft Store

Conservatory Stripe and Script Paper: Daisy D's

Swirl Paper: Scrap Ease

Olive Cardstock (for card): Paper Cuts

Vintage Collage Image: Paperbag Studios

Cherish Word Charm and Metal Art Frame: K&Company

Adhesives: UHU Glue Stick; Glue Dots International

Other: Vintage buttons

[INSTRUCTIONS]

Cut and fold olive cardstock to create a card. Cut and tear papers; glue to folded card. Attach metal frame to card over vintage image with Glue Dots. Adhere buttons and word charm to card with Glue Dots.

Gentle Inspiration

PATTI MUMA

[MATERIALS]

Music Notes and Dictionary Paper: K&Company
Black and Cream Cardstock: Local Craft Store
Sepia Archival Dye Inkpad: Ranger Industries
Black Plastic Slide Mount: Design Originals
Adhesives: Avery Glue Stick; Pop Dots
Other: Copy of vintage photo
Tools: Deckle scissors.

[INSTRUCTIONS]

1. Create a card from cream cardstock.

2. Using a deckle scissors trim black cardstock slightly smaller then card, layer on a cut strip of music paper; glue both to card.

3. Trim black and cream paper with deckle scissors. Layer papers and photo; attach to card.

4. Cut out dictionary definition of choice. Mount inside black slide mount.

5. Attach slide mount with Pop Dots adhesive foam.

Precious Notion

AMY WELLENSTEIN

[MATERIALS]

Brown Cardstock (for card): Bazzill

Cream Cardstock: Bazzill

Coffee Archival Dye Ink: Ranger Industries

Fabric Art (Photo): ARTchix Studio

"Safety Pin Border" Rubber Stamp: Stampotique Originals

Small Safety Pin: Metal Memorabilia by Li'l Davis Designs

Rectangle Zipper Pull "Precious": All My Memories

Metal Button: K&Company

Adhesives: The Ultimate! Glue; Scotch Double-Stick Tape

Other: Brown thread, osnaburg fabric and cotton batting

[INSTRUCTIONS]

1. Cut a square of osnaburg (burlap-like) fabric; fray the edges.

2. Cut a square of cotton batting smaller than the osnaburg.

3. Glue a fabric photo to the center of the osnaburg. Stuff with batting and use brown thread to sew a primitive stitch around the edges of the osnaburg to photo, sewing them together.

4. Glue the stuffed, layered fabric to a square of brown cardstock.

5. Glue a metal button on the lower left corner of the photo.

6. Use a small safety pin to attach a metal zipper pull "Precious" to the right side of the photo.

7. Stamp safety pin border around the edges of a square cream panel using coffee ink.

8. Layer all pieces onto a brown card.

Grandmother Card

AMY WELLENSTEIN

[MATERIALS]

Black Cardstock (for card): Bazzill

White Cardstock: Bazzill

Printed Text Paper: 7gypsies

"Woods" White Crackle Die Cut Frame: This & That division of My Mind's Eye

"Moments" Bubble Phrase: Li'l Davis Designs

Mica: USArtQuest

Brads: Making Memories

Oval Frame: Metal Memorabilia by Li'l Davis Designs

Adhesives: UHU Glue Stick; Scotch Double-Stick Tape; Embossable Tape Sheets by Amy's Magic

Other: Color copy of old photo

[INSTRUCTIONS]

1. Transfer a color copy of an old photo to a piece of mica using the mica transfer technique.*

2. Layer mica transfer on white cardstock.

3. Adhere the mica transfer to the back side of a die cut frame.

4. Glue small strips of patterned paper in place to frame the focal image. Attach brads at the corners.

5. Fold black cardstock to form a card. Use double-stick tape to attach the frame to the card.

6. Mount a bubble phrase in an oval frame and adhere to card.

*Mica transfer technique: This technique works with COLOR COPIES, not inkjet prints.)

1. Color copy a photograph.

2. Adhere double-stick tape sheet to the RIGHT side of the color copy. Burnish with a bone folder (to ensure good adhesion) then peel off the liner.

3. Adhere the color copy to a piece of mica (sandwiching the double-stick tape sheet in the middle).

4. Burnish again with a bone folder to ensure good adhesion.

5. Spritz the back of the color copy (which is attached to the mica) with water. Once the paper has softened, rub it off gently with your fingertip.

6. Periodically rinse the paper pulp off of the mica in a small bowl of water and continue to rub until all the paper has been removed. Only the toner will remain once the paper is rubbed off.

*"You don't take a
photograph, you make it."
- Ansel Adams*

Remember
AMY WELLENSTEIN

[MATERIALS]

White Cardstock (for card):
Bazzill

Ivory and Black Cardstock:
Bazzill

Defined Clear Stickers
("Vacation"):
Making Memories

"Narratives" Slide Mounts:
Creative Imaginations

Decorative Brads:
Making Memories

Adhesive:
Scotch Double-Stick Tape

Other: Photograph

[INSTRUCTIONS]

1. Cut and fold white cardstock to make card.

2. Encase a small photo in a slide mount.

3. Layer the slide mount onto black cardstock.

4. Layer a panel of ivory card stock onto black cardstock.

5. Attach decorative brads on all four corners.

6. Adhere the panel to a pre-made white card.

7. Attach the slide mount to the front of the card.

8. Adhere a clear sticker below the slide mount.

LOVE AMY WELLENSTEIN

[MATERIALS]

White Ancient Tile Paper: Paper Adventures

Black Cardstock (for card): Bazzill

Vellum: Local Craft Store

"Love" Transparency : Daisy D's Elements

Big Slide Mount: FoofaLa

Adhesives: Scotch Double-Stick Tape and Double-Stick Foam Tape

Other: Photograph and sandpaper

[INSTRUCTIONS]

1. Cut black cardstock and fold to make card.

2. Sand the surface of a large black slide mount to give it a distressed appearance.

3. Use black cardstock to create a narrow mat in the opening of the slide mount.

4. Adhere a piece of printed transparency and photo to the back of the slide mount frame.

5. Tear a small strip of vellum and adhere it to the back of a portion of the transparency.

6. Layer and glue all to pre-made black card.

DAY DREAMER
ROBEN-MARIE SMITH

[MATERIALS]

Red Floral Paper:
Li'l Davis Designs

Black Cardstock (for card):
Paper Cuts

Vintage Collage Image:
Paperbag Studios

Flower Swirl Washers:
American Tag

Adhesives: UHU Glue Stick;
Glue Dots International

Other: Black scrap paper
and old book paper

Tools: Star Punches
by Marvy Uchida

[INSTRUCTIONS]

Cut black cardstock and fold to make card. Cut and glue red floral scrap paper to front of folded black card. Cut defined word ("Dream") and glue to black paper; adhere to card. Tear page from old book and layer to black paper; glue to card. Cut out vintage images and glue to card. Glue small defined words to card over old book paper. Adhere black washers with Glue Dots. Using star punch, create a large black paper star and a smaller one out of printed word paper. Layer together and glue to card.

"Looking at the stars always makes me dream." ~ Vincent van Gogh

> "*I don't like formal gardens. I like wild nature. It's just the wilderness instinct in me, I guess.*"
> ~ Walt Disney

A Perfect Moment Card
ROBEN-MARIE SMITH

[MATERIALS]

Patterned Paper: Anna Griffin

Speckled Olive Cardstock (for card): Paper Cuts

Sticker Words: Color Oasis Phrases by EK Success

Ribbon: Local Craft Store

Metal Word Charm and Eyelet Flower: Making Memories

Adhesives: Glue Dots International; UHU Glue Stick; The Ultimate! Glue

Other: Vintage button and photograph

[INSTRUCTIONS]

Cut olive cardstock and fold to make card. Tear and glue patterned paper to folded card. Cut and mount picture and metal word onto olive cardstock pieces and glue to card. Adhere ribbon and glue to card at an angle across the picture. Adhere button and flower charm with Glue Dots. Peel and place sticker words on card as shown.

[MATERIALS]

Papers: 7gypsies

Tan Cardstock (for card): Paper Cuts

Dot Matrix Computer Paper: Local Office Supply

Clearly Yours Stitch Bubble Sticker: K&Company

Walnut Ink Crystals: FoofaLa

Jet Black StazOn Solvent Inkpad: Tsukineko

"Misunderstood" Rubber Stamp: Paperbag Studios

Black Beads: Local Craft Store

Black Photo Corners: Canson

Copper Frame: Li'l Davis Designs

Eyelets: Making Memories

Adhesives: UHU Glue Stick; Glue Dots International

Other: Vintage watch face

Tools: Spray bottle, eyelet setter and hammer

[INSTRUCTIONS]

Cut and tear papers and glue to folded tan card. Use black ink to stamp "Misunderstood" onto scrapbook paper; glue to page. Spritz computer paper with walnut ink mixed with distilled water. * Cut a piece of spritzed paper to glue to right side of card. Add eyelets to metal frame; use Glue Dots to adhere frame with watch face to card. Add beads to top corners with Glue Dots. Peel and stick stitched border and word definition to card as shown.

Using distilled water will extend the life of leftover stored walnut ink.

Joshua
ROBEN-MARIE SMITH

Grandparents Day Card
SARAH NORTHRUP

"Nobody can do for little children what grandparents do. Grandparents sort of sprinkle stardust over the lives of little children." ~ Alex Haley

[MATERIALS]

Pre-folded Cards: Local Craft Store

Floral and Postage Paper: K&Company

Shipping Tags: Local Craft Store

Grand Adhesion "Definition with Heart:" K&Company

"Love" Label: Pebbles, Inc.

Chestnut Roan Cat's Eye Fluid Chaulk Inkpad: Clearsnap

"Grandpa and Grandma" Button and Words on Acrylic: Junkitz

Oval Metal Frame with Charm: K&Company

Other: Vintage picture

Adhesives: The Ultimate! Glue; Yes! Paste

[INSTRUCTIONS]

1. Cut paper to size for background of pre-folded card and tag.

2. Adhere paper to card with Yes! Paste, let dry flat.

3. Rub edges of card, tag and string with chestnut roan ink to "age". Glue tag and string to card with the Ultimate! Glue. Press Grand Adhesion definition with heart onto tag.

4. Press "Love" label onto card.

5. Glue button and acrylic words to card using The Ultimate! Glue.

6. Place photo in frame and adhere to card with The Ultimate! Glue.

7. Cut a piece of plastic bubble wrap to size of card. Place over card and weight with book. Dry overnight.

Laughter
ROBEN-MARIE SMITH

[MATERIALS]

Script and Light Purple Text Paper: 7gypsies
Purple Paper: K&Company
Black Cardstock (for card): Paper Cuts
Rub-On Words: Making Memories
Sticker Word: K&Company
Jet Black StazOn Solvent Inkpad: Tsukineko
"Best Friends" Rubber Stamp: Paperbag Studios
Grand Adhesions Flowers: K&Company
Black Photo Corners: Canson
Silver Bead Spacers: Local Craft Store
Adhesives: UHU Glue Stick; Glue Dots International

[INSTRUCTIONS]

Cut and tear papers and glue to folded black card. Stamp "Best Friends" image with black dye ink onto purple paper. Cut out image, add black photo corners and adhere to card. Peel and adhere sticker word and flowers to card. Rub on "Laughter" at lower left corner. Adhere bead spacers to card with Glue Dots.

Boy in Toy Airplane

AMY WELLENSTEIN

[MATERIALS]

Brown Background Paper: The Paper Loft
Red Patterned Paper: 7gypsies
Black Cardstock: Bazzill
Puzzle Piece Stickers: Life's Journey by K&Company
"Travel" Transparency: by Daisy D's Elements
Boy in Airplane Image: Fabric Art by ARTchix Studio
Adhesives: Scotch Double-Stick Tape
Other: Slide mounts and ledger transparency

[INSTRUCTIONS]

1. Trim the fabric image to fit on the front of a slide mount.
2. Attach the image to the slide mount using double-stick tape.
3. Adhere another slide mount over the fabric image.
4. Attach two transparencies and two more slide mounts, alternating layers.
5. Cover a fifth slide mount with brown patterned paper and adhere it to the previous layers.
6. Layer brown patterned paper, red script paper and black cardstock on a black card.
7. Use double-stick tape to secure the slide mounts to the front of the card.
8. Embellish the slide mount frame with a puzzle piece sticker.

Best Buddies

JILL HAGLUND

"A man's growth is seen in the successive choirs of his friends."
~ Ralph Waldo Emerson

[MATERIALS]

Pre-folded Ivory Card: Local Craft Store
"Provence" Red Striped Paper: 7gypsies
Small Tag: K&Company
Letters and Numbers: K&Company
Metal Watch Face: K&Company
Adhesive: Yes! Paste; The Ultimate! Glue
Other: Coffee-dyed lace, script paper and photograph

[INSTRUCTIONS]

Cut and paste red striped paper to pre-folded card. Tear scrap of script paper and layer over top. Add photo. Cover with a piece of waxed paper, press with weight of heavy book and dry flat. Press adhesive letters ("dad"), numbers and tag to card. Glue watch face and lace border to card. Press and dry once more.

Sweet Abby
ROBEN-MARIE SMITH

[MATERIALS]

Ivory Cardstock (for card):
Local Craft Store

**Background, Crackle and
Heart Collage Papers:**
Daisy D's

"Childhood" Sticker Word:
Pebbles, Inc.

Letter Stickers: Rebecca
Sower Designs/EK Success

"Sweet" Word Sticker:
K&Company

Ticket: Anima Designs

Twine and Lace:
Local Craft Store

Metal Key: K&Company

Gold Clip: Local Office Supply

Adhesives: UHU Glue Stick;
Glue Dots International

Other: Vintage buttons,
photograph and game piece

[INSTRUCTIONS]

Cut and glue background
paper to folded ivory card. Tear
a piece of crackle paper and
glue to left side of card. Cut
out heart collage and photograph, glue both to card. Glue
lace and ticket to card. Use
Glue Dots to adhere buttons,
key and game piece.
Peel and place sticker
words and letters
as shown. Add
clip to side of card.

HELLO
FRIEND
TAG

AMY WELLENSTEIN

[MATERIALS]

Red Cardstock: Bazzill

Dictionary Circle Tags:
Real Life Cardstock Stickers by
Pebbles, Inc.

Large White Tag:
A Stamp in the Hand

Sepia Archival Dye Inkpad:
Ranger Industries

**Silver Encore Ultimate
Metallics and Red VersaFine
Inkpads:** Tsukineko

Rubber Stamps: "Safety Pin
Border," "Antique Border" and
Tall Alphabet by Stampotique
Originals

Metal Tape:
Local Hardware Store

"Love" Charm:
Blue Moon Beads
by Westrim Crafts

Twist Ties ("Love"):
I Kandee by Pebbles, Inc.

Red Safety Pin:
Li'l Davis Designs

Silver Safety Pin:
Local Craft Store

Clear Embossing Powder:
Ranger Industries

Adhesives: Xyron Machine;
UHU Glue Stick;
Scotch Foam Tape

Other: Photograph
and page from an old book

Tools: Heart Punch
by EK Success

[INSTRUCTIONS]

1. Use Xyron to adhere a cut out photograph to a large white tag.
2. Emboss safety pin border with silver ink and clear powder down the left side of the tag.
3. Use alphabet stamps and sepia ink to stamp "HELLO FRIEND" up the right side of the tag.
4. Stamp antique border in red ink on the top and bottom edges of the tag.
5. Adhere a round sticker to the upper right corner. Punch a heart from red cardstock and attach it to the round sticker with foam tape.
6. Use metal tape to create a small crown. Adhere the crown to the little girl. Cut a number from an old book page and adhere it to the crown.
7. Use safety pins to suspend a small word charm to the tag.
8. Twist a decorative twist tie through the hole on the tag.

[MATERIALS]

Background Paper (for card): K&Company

Mustard Cardstock: Paper Cuts

Vintage Collage Image: Paperbag Studios

Number Two Sticker: Li'l Davis Designs

Clearly Yours Stitched Border Sticker: K&Company

Fish Sticker: Karen Foster Design

Fine Tip Sharpie Marker: Local Office Supply

Beads: Local Craft Store

Metal Quote Charm: Making Memories

Adhesives: UHU Glue Stick; Glue Dots International

Other: Vintage book paper

[INSTRUCTIONS]

Cut and fold mustard cardstock into card. Cut and glue background paper to front of card. Tear vintage book page and glue to card front. Adhere fish sticker. Cut out vintage image of children and glue to card. Using marker, draw swirl lines as shown. Adhere buttons and metal word charm to card with Glue Dots. Peel and stick on number "2" and stitched border.

A Moment in Time
ROBEN-MARIE SMITH

Remember
ROBEN-MARIE SMITH

[MATERIALS]

Dark Brown Cardstock (for card): Local Craft Store

Map Paper: K&Company

Sticker Words: Karen Foster Design

Sticker Postage: Nostalgiques by Rebecca Sower/ EK Success

Transparency Film: Local Office Supply

Adhesives: UHU Glue Stick; Judi Kins Diamond Glaze

Other: Old book paper, old key game pieces, vintage photo and ledger paper

[INSTRUCTIONS]

Collage front of dark brown card base with map scrapbook paper and old papers and ledger. Adhere printed transparency to card with Diamond Glaze. Add sticker words and postage. Cut out and glue game piece numbers to front of transparency. Adhere old key to card with Glue Dots.

Secrets
ROBEN-MARIE SMITH

[MATERIALS]

Pre-folded Black Card: Paper Reflections by DMD Industries

Green Paper: Rebecca Sower Designs/ EK Success

Black Script Paper: 7gypsies

Quote Sticker: Color Oasis Phrases by EK Success

Printed Acetate: 7gypsies

Ribbon: Local Craft Store

Printed Twill: 7gypsies

Black Beads: Local Craft Store

Silver Button: K&Company

Silver Buckle, Silver Clip and Black Nail Heads: 7gypsies

Adhesives: UHU Glue Stick; Glue Dots International; Judi Kins Diamond Glaze

Other: Photograph

[INSTRUCTIONS]

Cut green paper and adhere to pre-folded black card. Tear script paper for top of card and cut a smaller piece for the side of the photo; glue both to card. Smear Diamond Glaze evenly on the back of the printed acetate and adhere to card. Attach wide green ribbon to the buckle with nail heads and glue to card, along with other ribbons. Adhere beads and button to card with Glue Dots. Peel and place the quote to the bottom right of the card.

Vintage Post
AMY WELLENSTEIN

"One should never travel by train or planes without one's diary."
~ Oscar Wilde

[MATERIALS]

Black Cardstock (for card): Bazzill

Stamp Stickers (Random): Real Life Cardstock Stickers by Pebbles, Inc.

Adhesive: Xyron Machine

Other: Photograph

[INSTRUCTIONS]

1. Adhere postage stamp stickers to the front of a black card, leaving a narrow border around the edges.

2. Trim out photo and apply Xyron adhesive to back of photograph.

3. Adhere photo to front of card.

London Tag

AMY WELLENSTEIN

[MATERIALS]

Large Shipping Tag: Local Craft Store or Office Supply

Thankful Words ("explore"), Forget Me Not Collage Sticker: Life's Journey by K&Company

"London" Transparency: 7gypsies

Sepia Archival Dye Inkpad: Ranger Industries

Ribbon: Local Craft Store

Brads: Making Memories

Adhesive: Xyron Machine

Other: Printed twill tape

[INSTRUCTIONS]

1. Sponge sepia ink along the edges of a large shipping tag.

2. Use Xyron to adhere a transparency image to the tag.

3. Embellish the tag with decorative stickers.

4. Use brads to attach a small strip of transparency to the upper right side.

5. Tie ribbon and printed twill tape through the hole on the card.

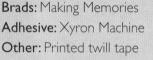

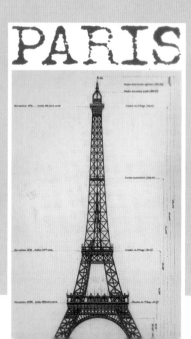

Paris Tag

AMY WELLENSTEIN

[MATERIALS]

Large Shipping Tag: Local Craft Store or Office Supply

Wood Block Type Alphabet: Life's Journey by K&Company

"Paris" Transparency: 7gypsies

Sepia Archival Dye Inkpad: Ranger Industries

Ribbon: Local Craft Store

Letterpress Twill ("journey"): 7gypsies

Label Tape ("travel"): Dymo Label Maker

Metal Art Tags ("dream"), Metal Bar and Copper Key: Life's Journey by K&Company

Jump Ring: Local Craft Store or Jewelry Supply

Adhesives: Xyron Machine; The Ultimate! Glue; Scotch Double-Stick Tape

Tools: Dymo Label Maker

[INSTRUCTIONS]

1. Sponge sepia ink along the edges of a large shipping tag.

2. Use Xyron to adhere a transparency image to the tag.

3. Embellish the tag with alphabet stickers, Dymo Label Maker tape word and a copper key.

4. Glue a metal bar across the top of the tag.

5. Use a jump ring to hold a metal tag on the bar. Adhere the small metal tag to the transparency using foam tape.

6. Tie ribbon and printed twill tape through the hole on the card.

Dream

ROBEN-MARIE SMITH

[MATERIALS]

Dark Blue Cardstock:
Local Craft Store

Botanical Print Paper:
K&Company

Clearly Yours Postage Sticker:
K&Company

Vintage Collage Image:
Paperbag Studios

Simply Stated Rub-On Words:
Making Memories

Metal Rimmed Tag:
Making Memories

Black Ancient Page Inkpad:
Clearsnap

Moonlight White Brilliance Inkpad:
Tsukineko

Swirl Rubber Stamp:
Renaissance Art Stamps

Old Writing Rubber Stamp:
Hero Arts

Silk Flower and Leaves:
Local Craft Store

Silver Mini Brad: Making Memories

Adhesives: UHU Glue Stick; Glue
Dots International

Other: Lace and buttons

[INSTRUCTIONS]

Cut and fold dark blue cardstock into card. Stamp the right edge of a dark blue folded card with script stamp in Moonlight White pigment ink. Tear and glue botanical print paper to the card. Glue vintage photo to card and adhere buttons with Glue Dots. Peel and stick bubble postage to the right bottom of the photo. Add a silver brad to the center of a silk flower and add flower and leaves to card with Glue Dots. Add rub-on words to metal rimmed tag and glue to card. Adhere lace flowers with Glue Dots.

Enduring Beauty

ROBEN-MARIE SMITH

[MATERIALS]

Tan Cardstock (for card):
LocalCraft Store

Papers: 7gypsies

Defined Word Definitions
and Rub-On Words:
Making Memories

Small White Jewelry Tags:
Local Office Supply

Transparency Image of Girl:
ARTchix Studio

Silk Flower and Ribbons:
Local Craft Store

Copper Frame: K&Company

Mini Brad and Safety Pin:
Making Memories

Gold Clip: Local Craft Store

Gold Tassel Charm: 7gypsies

Adhesives: UHU Glue Stick;
Glue Dots International;
Judi Kins Diamond Glaze

[INSTRUCTIONS]

Cut out and fold tan cardstock
into card. Cut background paper
and glue to folded tan card.
Smear Diamond Glaze to the
back of acetate and adhere to
card. Tie ribbons around card
and attach tags and gold tassel.
Glue word definition behind
mini frame and adhere to card
with Glue Dots. Add mini brad
to silk flower and glue to card.
Add clip to top of card, along
with a small tag. Glue wide
ribbon to bottom of card. Add
rub-on word at top right.

Forever Friends

ROBEN-MARIE SMITH

[MATERIALS]

Ivory Card Stock (for card): Local Craft Store

Stripe Paper: 7gypsies

Alphabet Paper: Daisy D's

Ivory Card Stock: Paper Cuts

Sticker Tab: 7 gypsies

Sticker Words: Making Memories

Vintage Collage Image: Paperbag Studios

Heart and Postage (cut from tags): Daisy D's

Ticket: Anima Designs

Fine Tip Black Marker: Local Office Supply

Trust Charm and Metal Rod: K&Company

Adhesives: UHU Glue Stick; Glue Dots International

Other: Vintage buttons and an old book page

[INSTRUCTIONS]

Cut, tear and glue papers to front of folded ivory card. Add sticker tab to top of photo; write "Friends" on it with marker; glue to card. Cut out postage and heart; glue to card. Peel and adhere sticker definition. Adhere vintage buttons with Glue Dots. Glue piece of ticket to card on top of old book scrap.

"Friends... they cherish one another's hopes. They are kind to one another's dreams."
~ Henry David Thoreau

AMY WELLENSTEIN

[MATERIALS]

Black Cardstock (for card): Bazzill

Light Blue Card Stock: Bazzill

Text Paper: 7gypsies

Metal Art Brass Alphabet: Life's Journey by K&Company

Magnolia Bud VersaMagic Inkpad: Tsukineko

Rubber Stamp "No. 074819": Limited Edition Rubberstamps

Gray Glass Effects Square (with opening): Heidi Grace Designs

Adhesives: UHU Glue Stick; Embossable Tape Sheets by Amy's Magic

Other: Photograph and ribbon

Tools: 1/8" hole punch

[INSTRUCTIONS]

1. Create a small square card from black cardstock.

2. Use a 1/8" hole punch to punch holes down the left and right sides of the card.

3. Line the front of the card with a square of light blue cardstock.

4. Line the Glass Effects Square with double-stick tape (embossable tape sheet).

5. Adhere text paper to the back of the square.

6. Adhere a small photo in the opening of the square.

7. Spell out the word "BOY" using adhesive-backed brass letters.

8. Use Magnolia Bud ink to stamp "No. 074819" across the bottom of the card.

9. Tie a ribbon with bow across the top of the card.

WISH YOU WERE

HERE

Parent (pē·rĕnt), a fa...

love (luv) *n.* [ME < ...
hold clo... your... art
...a d...
...ch

father

mother

...tion
Son (...
in rel...

WISH YOU WERE HERE

AMY WELLENSTEIN

[MATERIALS]
Antique Post: Daisy D's
Brown Patterned Paper: The Paper Loft
Vintage Sepia and Onyx Black VersaFine Inkpads: Tsukineko
Rubber Stamps: "Travel," "Vacation" and "Photos" by Stampotique Originals
Slide Mount Holder: Local Craft Store
Metal Frame: Marcella by Kay
Adhesives: UHU Glue Stick; Scotch Double-Stick Tape
Other: Photographs
Tools: Label Maker by Dymo

[INSTRUCTIONS]
1. Cover slide mount holder with patterned paper.
2. Adhere a metal frame and photograph to the front cover of the holder.
3. Use label maker to emboss "WISH YOU WERE HERE." Adhere to the frame.
4. Stamp "Travel" on the left side of the front cover using Vintage Sepia ink.
5. Stamp "Vacation" and "Photos" on the inside of the cover using Onyx Black ink.
6. Use label maker to emboss date; adhere to the inside of the cover.
7. Use double-stick tape to attach photos to the inserts.

HANGING CARD

AMY WELLENSTEIN

[MATERIALS]
Cream Cardstock: Bazzill
"Friend Rouge" and "Friend Cream" Papers: 7gypsies
Butterfly Wings: Finmark "Butterflies" Design Paper
"Love" Transparency: Daisy D's Elements
Chain (Nickel Toggles #1): Karen Foster Metals
Black Slide Mounts: Local Craft Store
Adhesives: UHU Glue Stick; Scotch Double-Stick Tape
Other: Photograph and sandpaper

"My favorite thing is to go where I've never been."
- Diane Arbus

[INSTRUCTIONS]
1. Adhere wings and words to a small photo using glue stick.
2. Layer the photo and transparency between several slide mounts to create depth. Line the back slide mount with cream patterned paper.
3. Adhere brown patterned paper to the front of a slide mount. Sand to create a distressed appearance.
4. Attach the sanded slide mount to the front of the other mounts, sandwiching the ends of a small chain between the layers.
5. Create a small card from cream cardstock to fit on the back of the slide mount.

Legacy

AMY WELLENSTEIN

[MATERIALS]

Brown Cardstock (for card):
Bazzill

Black Cardstock: Bazill

Patterned Paper: 7gypsies

Oval Script Alphabet:
Life's Journey by K&Company

Laminate Film:
Local Office Supply

Wooden Number:
Li'l Davis Designs

Waxed Linen Cord:
Local Craft Store

Steel Ends: 7gypsies

Silver Eyelets: Making Memories

Silver Paper Fasteners:
Local Office Supply

Adhesives: UHU Glue Stick;
Scotch Double-Stick Tape

Other: Photograph

[INSTRUCTIONS]

1. Use brown cardstock to make a card.

2. Adhere striped paper to the front of the card.

3. Use clear laminating film to create a transfer from a photo.*

4. Line the photo with architectural patterned paper and layer onto black cardstock.

5. Adhere the transfer to the front of the card.

6. Use alphabet stickers to spell out "LEGACY" on a strip of black cardstock.

7. Use eyelets, steel ends, paper fasteners and waxed linen cord to secure the strip to the right side of the card.

* See page 51 for technique instruction.

Bejeweled Baby

AMY WELLENSTEIN

[MATERIALS]

Black Cardstock (for card):
Bazzill

Cranberry Leaf Damask Paper: Sonnets by Sharon Soneff for Creative Imaginations

Bits & Pieces Stickers (Love): Real Life Cardstock Stickers by Pebbles, Inc.

Jeweled Label Holder: Local Craft Store

Silver Buckle (Plastic): Li'l Davis Designs

Metal Frame: Making Memories

Adhesives: The Ultimate! Glue; Scotch Double-Stick Tape and Foam Mounting Tape

Other: Photograph and chipboard

[INSTRUCTIONS]

1. Adhere a square piece of red paper to a black card.

2. Adhere a metal frame to the center of the red panel using double-stick tape.

3. Glue a silver buckle in the center of the frame.

4. Reinforce a photograph with chipboard and trim; adhere to the center of the buckle using double-stick foam mounting tape.

5. Glue a jeweled label holder below the red panel.

6. Adhere the word "LOVE" in the window of the label holder.

In a Word

ROBEN-MARIE SMITH

[MATERIALS]

Checkered Paper: Daisy D's
Letter Paper: 7gypsies
White Computer Paper:
Local Office Supply
Vintage Collage Image:
Paperbag Studios
Bubble Letters:
Li'l Davis Designs
Manila Tag: Local Office Supply
Printed Acetate: Daisy D's
Walnut Ink: Local Craft Store
Ribbon: Local Craft Store
Black Photo Corners: Canson
Silver Charm: 7gypsies
Adhesives: UHU Glue Stick;
Glue Dots International;
Judi Kins Diamond Glaze
Tools: Spray bottle

[INSTRUCTIONS]

Cut and glue checkered paper to pre-folded card. Spritz white computer paper with walnut ink mixed with water; let dry and layer to card. Smear Diamond Glaze on back of printed acetate and adhere to card. Adhere bubble letters to card with Glue Dots. Cover manila tag with alphabet paper; add ribbons and silver charm. Attach black photo corners to photo and glue it to the tag. Adhere tag to card.

"Enlightenment takes place when one lets his innocence emerge and sees nature and life with a childlike awe and respect."
- Charles Duback

[MATERIALS]

Brown Cardstock (for card):
Bazzill

Le Fleur Lavender Paper:
K&Company

Catherine's Memoir:
Sandylion Sticker Designs

Dictionary Definitions ("lovely"): FoofaLa

Brianna Letters & Die Cuts:
K&Company

Metal Frame: Scrapworks

Adhesives: UHU Glue Stick

Other: Photograph

[INSTRUCTIONS]

1. Adhere a photo to the back of a small metal frame.

2. Attach frame to a panel of script patterned paper.

3. Embellish the panel with alphabet stickers and flower stickers.

4. Attach the panel to a piece of lavender paper, mount on a brown card.

5. Trim the word "lovely" from a cardstock dictionary definition and glue it to the frame.

Happy Days

AMY WELLENSTEIN

Lucky To Be Your Friend

PATTI MUMA

[MATERIALS]

Background Paper: 7gypsies

Typewriter Letter Stickers:
Nostalgiques by Rebecca Sower/EK Success

Cream-Colored Tag: FoofaLa

Sepia Archival Dye Inkpad: Ranger Industries

Black and Brown Inks: Marvy Matchables

Walnut Ink: Postmodern Design

Rubber Stamps: Key by Stampin' Up!
and Postal Mark by Hero Arts

Ribbon: 7gypsies

Black Photo Corners: Canson

Adhesive: Glue Stick

Other: Vintage Bingo card and copy
of vintage photograph

Tools: Fiskars 12-inch Paper Cutter,
spray bottle, sponge and fine grade sandpaper

[INSTRUCTIONS]

1. Cut background paper to size and glue to card. Smooth out all wrinkles. Set aside and press to dry flat.

2. Spray Bingo card with walnut stain and press to dry flat. Once dry, add typewriter stickers to Bingo card. Set aside.

3. Tear copy of vintage photograph along edges, sponge them with sepia ink and glue onto walnut-stained cardstock. Trim. Set aside.

3. Stamp cream-colored tag in random pattern with chosen stamps. Sponge sepia ink around edge of tag.

4. Attach prepared vintage photograph to front of tag using black photo corners. Add ribbon to top of tag.

5. Assemble card by gluing down Bingo card, then layer tag on the top.

With this Ring Wedding Card

PATTI MUMA

[MATERIALS]

London Map Paper: K&Company

Tan Cardstock(for card): Local Craft Store

Large Tag and Circular Tag: Local Craft Store or Office Supply

Grand Adhesion Button Border Sticker: Life's Journey by K&Company

Nostalgic Print Tag: FoofaLa

Small Metal-Rimmed Tag: Local Office Supply

Sepia Archival Dye Inkpad: Ranger Industries

Palm Leaf Inkpad: Ancient Page by Clearsnap

Terra Cotta and Black Inks: Marvy Matchables

Typewriter Style Letters Rubber Stamp: Hero Arts

Ribbons: EK Success and Offray

Eyelet: Making Memories

Adhesives: Glue Stick; Adhesive Glitter by Ranger Industries; Super Bond Glue

Other: Faux wedding rings, paper doily sprayed with walnut ink and copy of vintage picture

Tools: Fiskars 12-inch Paper Cutter, sponge, eyelet setter, hammer and craft knife

[INSTRUCTIONS]

1. Cut tan cardstock to desired size and fold to make card. Sponge card with various inks to age.

2. Adhere doily to bottom right corner of card and trim excess.

3. Sponge metal-rimmed tag with various inks and stamp "love" in center. Add a light coat of glitter glue to circle tag and allow to dry.

4. Collage pieces of map paper and photo to tag; sponge the edges for aging effect. Glue large tag to card.

5. Use glue stick to adhere circle tag to larger tag.

6. Add button border, rings and ribbon.

[MATERIALS]

Patterned Background Papers: Anna Griffin

Small Framed Drawing of Children: 7gypsies

Vintage Collage Image and Gold Paper Border: ARTchix Studio

Printed French Ribbon: Stamper's Anonymous

Other Ribbons: Local Craft Store

Twill: 7gypsies

Gold Triangle Clip: 7gypsies

Metal Label Holder: Making Memories

Upholstery Tack: Local Craft Store

Adhesives: Glue Stick; Glue Dots International; Clear Scotch Tape

[INSTRUCTIONS]

Cut and glue green patterned background papers to pre-folded card. Tie ribbon through holes in metal label. Add image of children behind label and adhere to card. Pull ribbons to back and tape in place. Glue gold paper border to the center of card. Attach clip to image and adhere to card. Glue French ribbon to the top of solid twill and adhere both to card. Remove end from tack and attach to card with a Glue Dot.

Joie de Vivre

ROBEN-MARIE SMITH

Michelangelo's Stairway
PATTI MUMA

[MATERIALS]

Cream Cardstock (for card):
Local Craft Store

Brown Background Paper:
7gypsies

Ledgers and Scripts Background Paper: K&Company

"This Place" Collage Transparency: ARTchix Studio

Sepia Archival Dye Inkpad:
Ranger Industries

Terra Cotta Inkpad:
Marvy Matchables

Eyelets: Making Memories

Adhesives: Glue Stick

Tools: Fiskars 12-inch Paper Cutter, sponge, scissors, hammer and eyelet setting tools

[INSTRUCTIONS]

1. Cut and fold card from white cardstock.

2. Sponge edges of white card with sepia and terra cotta inks.

3. Cut brown background paper to fit card and glue to card.

4. Trim transparency. Trim script background paper slightly larger. Use eyelets to attach and mount transparency to background paper.

5. Attach mounted transparency to card front.

6. Computer-generate text and print onto cream cardstock. Tear around the edges and sponge with inks. Adhere to card.

"My soul can find no staircase to heaven unless it be through Earth's loveliness."
~Michelangelo

Tell Me

PATTI MUMA

[MATERIALS]

Caramel Cardstock (for card): Local Craft Store

Script Kraft Paper: K&Company

Vintage Woman Transparency: ARTchix Studio

Sepia Archival Dye Inkpad: Ranger Industries

Eyelets and Brads: Local Craft Store

Adhesive: Glue Stick

Other: Ribbon

Tools: Fiskars 12-inch Paper Cutter, sponge, eyelet setter, hammer and awl

[INSTRUCTIONS]

1. Cut cardstock to desired size and fold to a card.

2. Cut script background paper to fit, glue onto card and lightly sponge edge with sepia ink.

3. Set eyelets on right edge of card front. Lace ribbon through holes and tie in bow.

4. Arrange transparency on the front of the card. Carefully poke holes through both transparency and card with awl. Attach transparency with brads.

London Adventure
PATTI MUMA

[MATERIALS]

White Pre-folded Card: Local Craft Store

Background Vellum: K&Company

Bubble Phrase: Li'l Davis Designs

Small Tag: Office Supply Store

"Big Ben" Transparency: 7gypsies

Sepia Archival Dye Inkpad: Ranger Industries

Walnut Ink: Postmodern Design

Black Waxed Cord: 7gypsies

Gold Brads: Local Craft Store

Small Oval Metal Frame and Bubble Phrase: Li'l Davis Designs

Adhesive: Glue Stick

Other: Small Scrabble tiles, beads and walnut-stained paper made from manila file folder

Tools: Fiskars 12-inch Paper Cutter, scissors, spray bottle, sponge and small awl

[INSTRUCTIONS]

1. Stain tag with walnut ink; let dry.
2. Press adhesive bubble phrase into oval. Glue onto tag.
3. Use black waxed cord to string on beads and tag. Set aside.
4. Cut background vellum to size and attach to front of card with gold brads.
5. Poke a hole in left-hand corner with awl. Run the waxed cord with beads and tag through the upper left-hand corner hole. Adjust to desired length; add brad to secure. Allow tag to dangle freely along side outer edge of card.

6. Cut walnut-stained paper and Big Ben transparency to size and attach both to card using gold brads.
7. Cut the Scrabble tiles, spell out "London" and glue word to card.

Remember Paris
PATTI MUMA

[MATERIALS]

Brown Cardstock: Local Craft Store

Sticker Phrase: Real Life by Pebbles, Inc.

"Woman" Transparency: ARTchix Studio

Sepia Archival Dye Inkpad: Ranger Industries

Brown, Dark Brown and Ochre Inkpads: Marvy Matchables

Palm Leaf Inkpad: Ancient Page by Clearsnap

Walnut Ink: Postmodern Design

"Paris" Rubber Stamp: Stampin' Up!

Eiffel Tower and Romeo and Juliet Text Rubber Stamps: Local Craft Store

Black Waxed Cord: 7gypsies

Metal Charm ("dream"): Local Craft Store

Adhesives: Glue Stick; Foam Mounting Tape

Other: Beads, page from an old French novel

Tools: Fiskars 12-inch Paper Cutter, spray, sponge and awl

[INSTRUCTIONS]

1. Cut brown cardstock to desired size and fold in a card.
2. Age book page with a sponge and various inks. Glue to card at an angle.
3. Stamp the Eiffel Tower image to upper right-hand corner. Leave enough space around the image for the black waxed cord.
4. Using the awl, poke holes, as seen on card. Thread waxed cord through the top, starting on the outside and weaving in and up.
5. Next, string the cord with a few beads, the charm and more beads.
6. Next, weave the cord down through the opposite holes, back up and out, tying a knot to secure.
7. Use a tiny piece of foam mounting tape to secure charm if desired.

Children's Legacy
ROBEN-MARIE SMITH

[MATERIALS]

Prefolded Card: Local Craft Store

Background Paper: 7gypsies

Ticket Paper: K&Company

Sticker Words: Making Memories

Printed Acetate: ARTchix Studio

Adhesives: UHU Glue Stick; Glue Dots International; Judi Kins Diamond Glaze

Other: Vintage buttons and photograph

[INSTRUCTIONS]

Cut and glue background paper to folded card. Smear Diamond Glaze to the back of printed acetate and adhere to front. Cut out children from photograph and ticket and glue to card. Adhere buttons with Glue Dots. Peel and place sticker words to card as shown.

"The greatest gift is a portion of thyself." - Ralph Waldo Emerson

legacy (leg´-e-se) something passed through a family, handed down as from an ancestor

cherish

[MATERIALS]

Buttons and Script Paper: K&Company

Tan Cardstock (for card), White Cardstock and Oval Photo Frame: Local Craft Store

Sticker Phrase "Mother" and Grand Adhesions Floral and Button Border Stickers: Life's Journey by K&Company

Sepia Archival Dye Inkpad: Ranger Industries

Terra Cotta, Ochre and Brilliant Yellow Inkpads: Marvy Matchables

Adhesive: Glue Stick

Other: Copy of vintage photograph

Tools: Sponges

[INSTRUCTIONS]

Cut and fold a card from tan cardstock. Cut script paper slightly smaller and attach to card. Sponge inks onto front of card and script paper to age. Add adhesive dimensional Button Border to side and bottom. Sponge oval frame with inks and glue photo in place. Cut buttons from Button paper, glue to frame as shown. Press adhesive floral stickers and sticker phrase to frame. Attach frame to card.

Mother's Gentle Beauty

PATTI MUMA

Christmas Ornament Card
AMY WELLENSTEIN

[MATERIALS]

Red Card Stock: Bazzill

Metallic Gold Cardstock: Local Craft Store

Rubber Stamps: design image by Magenta

Embossing Powder and Ink (Gold):
Local Craft Store

Thin Gold Wire: Local Craft Store

Adhesives: Scotch Thick
Double-Stick Tape

Tools: Pinking shears, embossing
heat tool

[INSTRUCTIONS]

1. Fold red cardstock in half. Cut out a round shaped card (be sure to leave an inch or so of the fold in tact).

2. Use any large *design type image* rubberstamp to stamp the background over the entire card using gold embossing ink.

3. Emboss stamped image on card using gold embossing ink powder and embossing heat tool.

4. Cut a strip of metallic gold cardstock (1/2" wide). Cut one edge using pinking shears. Cut off a one inch section to be used for the top of the ornament as an "ornament hanger."

5. Bend a small piece of gold wire into a loop. Secure the wire to the gold "ornament hanger", then to the top of the card using thick double stick tape.

Nested Ornaments Card
AMY WELLENSTEIN

[MATERIALS]

Black, Maroon, Dark Green and Medium Green Cardstock: Bazzill

Metallic Gold Cardstock: Local Craft Store

Currant Adirondack Dye Inkpad: Ranger Industries

Platinum MetalExtra Inkpad: Clearsnap

Encore Ultimate Metallic Gold: Tsukineko

Cloud White VersaMagic Inkpad: Tsukineko

Rubber Stamps: #26-019R by Magenta; Snowflakes by Stampendous; "Christmas Mosaic," "Merry Christmas," "Fax to Wolfgang (Large)," "Stencil Background" and "Olive Rose" by Stampotique Originals Stitched Leaves #22465 by Judikins; Italian Text by Rubber Baby Buggy Bumpers

Thin Gold Wire: Local Craft Store

Adhesives: UHU Glue Stick; Scotch Thick Double-Stick Tape

Embossing Powder (Brass and Clear): PSX

Tools: Pinking shears; large, medium, and small circle punches and embossing heat tool

[INSTRUCTIONS]

1. Accordion fold black cardstock; stamp "Snowflakes" using Cloud White ink.

2. Emboss "Merry Christmas" using gold pigment ink, clear powder and an embossing heat tool.

3. Use large, medium, and small circle punches to punch "ornaments" from green and maroon cardstock (note that two shades of green cardstock were used).

4. Stamp and/or emboss the circles using a variety of inks and images.

5. Cut a strip of metallic gold cardstock (1/2" wide); cut one edge using pinking shears, then cut off small sections (these will be used as "ornament hangers").

6. Bend several small pieces of gold wire into loops; secure the wires and hangers to the top of the ornaments using thick double-stick tape.

7. Use glue stick to adhere the ornaments to the card.

You're In My Thoughts

PATTI MUMA

[MATERIALS]

Black Cardstock (for card): Local Craft Store

Vintage Woman Transparency and "Letters and Ledgers" Collage Sheet: ARTchix Studio

Corner Sticker: K&Company

Sepia Archival Dye Inkpad: Ranger Industries

Brads: Local Craft Store

Adhesive: Glue Stick; Pop Dots

Other: Piece of script paper

Tools: Fiskars 12-inch Paper Cutter, sponge for inks, scissors and an awl

[INSTRUCTIONS]

Cut black cardstock to desired size and fold to a card. Cut large collage element from collage sheet and lightly sponge edges, glue to card. Cut and mat four small postcards from collage sheet and glue as shown. Cut and trim transparency. Attach the transparency to a piece of script paper by piercing both with an awl and adding brads. Attach matted transparency to the card using Pop Dots.

Hold Dear

ROBEN-MARIE SMITH

[MATERIALS]

Papers: Daisy D's

Brown Cardstock (for card):
Paper Cuts

Dot Matrix Computer Paper:
Local Office Supply

Vintage Collage and Old Ticket Collage Images: Paperbag Studios

Defined Words:
Making Memories

White Jewelry Tags:
Local Office Supply

Walnut Ink: Local Craft Store

Safety Pins: Making Memories

Adhesives: UHU Glue Stick;
Glue Dots International

Other: Vintage buttons and film negative

Tools: Stapler and spray bottle

[INSTRUCTIONS]

Cut and fold brown cardstock into a card. Cut, tear and glue paper in collage fashion to front of card. Cut out and glue defined words to card and to jewelry tags. Attach tags to card with safety pins. Cut out ticket and glue to card. Use Glue Dots to adhere buttons. Spritz computer paper with walnut ink and water; tear and layer to card with scrapbook papers, ticket and vintage photo stapled to card. Add all embellishments.

Vintage Book Card

AMY WELLENSTEIN

[MATERIALS]

Book Patterned Paper: Autumn Leaves
Cream Cardstock (for card): Bazzill
Rub-On Metallics: Craf-T Products, Inc.
Metal Art (Round Metal Frame): Life's Journey by K&Company
Metal Message ("generations"): Li'l Davis Designs
Adhesive: UHU Glue Stick
Other: Photograph

[INSTRUCTIONS]

1. Cut a section of Book Patterned paper and adhere it to a pre-folded cream-colored card.

2. Apply gold metallic rub-ons to a copper frame.

3. Center the frame over a photograph and adhere to card.

4. Adhere "generations" below the frame.

Product Resource Guide

3M / Scotch: www.scotchbrand.com

7gypsies: www.7gypsies.com

A Stamp in the Hand Co.: www.astampinthehand.com

All My Memories: www.allmymemories.com

American Art Clay Company, Inc.: www.amaco.com

American Tag: www.americantag.net

Amy's Magic: Local Craft Store

Angy's Dreams: www.angysdreams.it

Anima Designs: www.animadesigns.com

Anna Griffin: www.annagriffin.com

ARTchix Studio: www.artchixstudio.com

Autumn Leaves: www.autumnleaves.com

Avery Dennison Corporation: www.avery.com

Bazzill Basics Paper: www.bazzillbasics.com

Bo-Bunny Press: www.bobunny.com

Canson: www.canson.com

Carolee's Creations: www.caroleescreations.com

Clearsnap, Inc.: www.clearsnap.com

Color Oasis: www.stickopotamus.com

Craf-T Products: www.craf-tproducts.com

Crafter's Pick: www.crafterspick.com

Creative Imaginations: www.cigift.com

C-Thru Ruler: www.cthruruler.com

Daisy D's Paper Co: www.daisydspaper.com

DCC Technologies: www.dcctek.com

Delta: www.deltacrafts.com

Design Originals: www.d-originals.com

DMD Industries: www.dmdind.com

Dover Clipart: www.doverpublications.com

Dymo: www.dymo.com

E-6000 Craft Adhesive/Eclectic Products: 1-800-767-4667

EK Success: www.eksuccess.com

Ever After Scrapbook Company: www.addictedtoscrapbooking.com until www.everafterscrapbook.com is available

Fiskars: www.fiskars.com

FoofaLa: 1-800-588-6707; www.foofala.com

Fred B. Mullett: www.fredbmullett.com

Glue Dots International LLC: www.gluedots.com

Heidi Grace Designs: Local Craft Store

Hermafix: 1-888-CENTIS-6

Hero Arts: www.heroarts.com

Hyko Products: Local Craft Store

Judi Kins: www.judikins.com

Junkitz: www.junkitz.com

K&Company: www.kandcompany.com

Karen Foster Design: www.karenfosterdesign.com

Lala's Land by Lesley Riley: www.lalasland.com

Li'l Davis Designs: www.lildavisdesigns.com

Limited Edition Rubber Stamps: www.limitededitionrubberstamps.com

Lost Art Editions: Local Craft Store

Magenta: www.magentarubberstamps.com

Don't Forget to Check Your Local Craft Store for Supplies!

Product Resource Guide Continued

Making Memories: www.makingmemories.com

Marcella by Kay: Local Craft Store

Marvy Uchida: www.uchida.com

Midori: Local Craft Store

My Mind's Eye: www.frame-ups.com

My Sentiments Exactly: www.sentiments.com

Offray: www.offray.com

Paper Adventures: www.paperadventures.com

Paper Company, The: www.thepaperco.com

Paper Cuts:
www.papercutsthescrapbookstore.com

Paper Loft: www.paperloft.com

Paper Parachute: Local Craft Store

Paper Patch: www.paperpatch.com

Paperbag Studios: www.paperbagstudios.com

Pebbles Inc.: www.pebblesinc.com

Penny Black Rubber Stamps:
www.pennyblackinc.com

Pioneer: www.pioneerphotoalbums.com

Plaid Enterprises, Inc.: www.plaidonline.com

Postmodern Designs: 405-321-3176

Provo Craft: www.provocraft.com

Prym-Dritz Corporation: www.dritz.com

PSX: www.psxdesign.com

Raindrops on Roses: 919-845-1242

Ranger Industries, Inc.: www.rangerink.com

Renaissance Art Stamps: 860-485-7761

River City Rubberworks:
www.rivercityrubberworks.com

Rubber Baby Buggy Bumpers:
www.rubberbaby.com

Rubbermoon Stamp Company:
www.rubbermoon.com

Rusty Pickle: www.rustypickle.com

Sandylion Sticker Designs: www.sandylion.com

Scrap Ease: 1-800-274-3874

Sissix: www.sissix.com

Sobo Craft & Fabric Glue:
www.deltacrafts.com

St. Louis Trim: Local Craft Store

Stampendous: www.stampendous.com

Stampers Anonymous:
www.stampersanonymous.com

Stampin' Up!: www.stampinup.com

Stampington & Company:
www.stampington.com

Stampotique Originals:
www.stampotique.com

Suze Weinberg: www.schmoozewithsuze.com

Sweetwater: www.sweetwaterscrapbook.com

Treasure Cay: home.tampabay.rr.com/tcayarts

Tsukineko: www.tsukineko.com

USArtQuest, Inc.: www.usartquest.com

Vintage Charmings:
www.vintagecharmings.com

Wasau: Local Craft Store

Westrim Crafts: www.westrimcrafts.com

Wordsworth: www.wordsworthstamps.com

Xyron: www.xyron.com

Yes! Paste / Gane Brothers:
www.ganebrothers.com